MW00649282

FAITH OF OUR FATHERS

Faith
OF
Our Fathers

*A Brief History of Catholic Traditionalism
in the United States,
from Triumph to Traditionis Custodes*

STUART CHESSMAN

Foreword by
Peter A. Kwasniewski

Angelico Press

For information, address:
Angelico Press, Ltd.
169 Monitor St.
Brooklyn, NY 11222
www.angelicopress.com

ppr 978-1-62138-814-2
cloth 978-1-62138-815-9
ebook 978-1-62138-816-6

Cover photograph:
Allison Girone
Book and cover design:
Michael Schrauzer

Table of Contents

Foreword

THE LAST WEEKS OF JULY 2021 WERE HIGHLY emotional ones for many Catholics. We felt anger, and justifiably so, after a supreme pontiff who could never be called a guardian of tradition released *Traditionis Custodes*. We talked incessantly about what had happened, about what might happen in the future, about how we could respond, and about the meaning of it all.

Sooner or later, the initial shock wore off and the anger subsided. Other feelings crept in: sadness, depression, despondency, lethargy—or, worst of all, a desire to give up. One could see on social media the difference between the cholerics and the melancholics, between the tireless confronters and the worn-out pewsitters. The choleric will keep fighting until his last breath, but the melancholic might shrug his shoulders and say: "Oh well, I guess now that the pope has given my bishop the power to kill the Mass, and my bishop has killed it, I should just start going to the most reverent Novus Ordo I can find in a half-hour radius, and put up with the mediocre music and the multitudinous lay ministers. It's over: the TLM is dead. Our movement has been sunk and we should get on with life." Some even tried to persuade themselves that they were mistaken to be in love with the great Catholic tradition—that they must have been "too attached" to it for their own good, and that this must be Providence's way of purging them.

This is not the Spirit of God speaking: "for God gave us a spirit not of fear but of power and love and self-control"

(2 Tim 1:7). Certain ways of talking to ourselves are the voice of discouragement that casts down and does not lift up, a voice turning us away from the glory God has revealed to us to draw us closer to Himself *and* to help rebuild His fallen Church. In every traditionalist heart has been planted a seed of awakening and awareness, of wonder and gratitude, that is meant to grow and bear abundant fruits in oneself and for others, "for the perfecting of the saints, unto the work of ministering, unto the building up of the body of Christ" (Eph. 4:12). We must not walk away from that "glory streaming from heaven afar," or plunge into a tailspin that profits neither ourselves nor those around us.

How was it that the Tridentine Mass and other traditional practices and customs ended up in *our* lives, in this third decade of the twenty-first century? Why are they still here when, over fifty years ago, Paul VI tried to suppress nearly the whole liturgical legacy of Catholicism? How could a pope who was riding high on centuries of ultramontanism have failed to succeed in his ambition?

There was one reason, and one reason alone: our forefathers in the traditionalist movement resisted, protested, made sacrifices, and labored mightily to keep the patrimony of the Church alive when its appointed guardians were either indifferent to or actively expelling it. These men and women wore out the steps of bishops' houses and chanceries. They published pamphlets and gave talks, traveled to conferences, kept in touch internationally when doing so was more laborious than it is for us, sent representatives to knock on doors in Rome. They never stopped. The holy stubbornness of the first traditionalists, their unbending determination, their refusal to take no for an answer, is what rescued the Mass (and much else besides) and allowed it to reach you and me today.

Will we do the same for our children and grandchildren, for Catholics in the distant future? Right now, *we* are the links in the living chain of transmission. If there is to be a *Summorum Pontificum II* (or something even better) down the road, *we* will be responsible for the conditions of its possibility by refusing to go away, refusing to let the Church hierarchy tread on us.

Few who attend the TLM in our times—especially young people and young families—are well acquainted with the long-drawn-out battle to save the Latin Mass against unbelievable odds, with scarcely any resources, motley troops, and precious few leaders. We need to know our history. That is why the present short book by Stuart Chessman is so important and timely.

From the start of the traditionalist movement in the mid-1960s when the Mass began to be tampered with in earnest, a minority of concerned Catholics sought to retain the great ecclesiastical traditions: Latin, Gregorian chant, celebration *ad orientem*, full ceremonial, appropriate vestments, the complex theologico-liturgical body of Catholic prayer refined and matured over the centuries. The publication of Paul VI's Apostolic Constitution *Missale Romanum* in 1969—a document named more subtly, but no more truthfully, than Francis's Apostolic Letter *Traditionis Custodes*—galvanized the nascent movement, which shifted from defending this or that quality of traditional worship to defending the totality of the heritage embodied in the previous liturgical books (the *lex orandi*), including the doctrine they express (the *lex credendi*) and the way of life they support (the *lex vivendi*).

Throughout the 1970s and into the 1980s, it was a desperate uphill battle. Literate laymen, asking for a few crumbs from the master's table, vied against powerful bishops and cardinals who, as often as not, slammed the

door in their faces. Petitions were written up and signed,
frequently to no avail. Letters were published again and
again in newspapers and magazines. If not ignored, these
letters were treated to humiliating and condescending
replies from diocesan liturgists: "You'll get used to the
new Mass and soon love it!" (We're hearing similar things
today from well-meaning Catholics who just don't get it.)
It didn't matter that the traditionalists always had the better
arguments, as we see in the episode of William F. Buckley
Jr.'s *Firing Line* with Michael Davies and Malachi Martin;
they had no power, no position, no credibility, no numbers.

An elderly Englishman who lived through the revolution
shared with me the following memories:

> Now that the Traditional Latin Mass is under
> direct threat from a pope, it might be a good
> time to make the younger generation who are the
> majority in TLM parishes aware of the history
> of the Latin Mass movement and the seemingly
> impossible struggles in those early days when all
> did seem lost. It is indeed an unsettling time right
> now, and one which I thought we had put behind
> us. I started to serve Mass in 1952 and was in my
> twenties when the changes started to be imposed.
> I loved the Mass and Benediction and could
> not believe what was happening; it was as if the
> Church had gone mad. In the 1960s it seemed
> that all the young people were into drugs of all
> kinds—LSD, for example. I was approached on
> a number of occasions to "see if I was interested."
> My reply was always the same: the only drug I
> needed was incense; nothing else came close. I
> was usually met with incomprehension.
>
> During the very bleak days of the 1970s and
> 80s, I witnessed the wanton destruction of lovely
> parish churches but I was a voice crying in the
> wilderness—to coin a phrase—in my parish and
> diocese. Priests and altar servers were warned

against fraternizing with me; a bishop told me
my constant criticism of the Church's liturgy
would drive my family away from the practice of
their religion. Under the English Indult we were
granted three Masses *per year* at a country parish
on a Wednesday evening at 7:30 p.m., *with no
advertising.* On one occasion we asked for another
because a special feast of some English martyrs
fell on a Wednesday. The Bishop was very angry
and said that if we did not stop pressuring him
he would stop the lot!

I met Michael Davies in 1980 and we became
regular correspondents and eventually great friends.
In the 1980s a thaw started and the temperature
kept gradually improving until 2007 when the sun
finally came out. This scandalous document from
our current pontiff (isn't a pontiff supposed to be
a "bridge builder"?) is doomed to fail and there
are early positive signs that it will. Any senior
prelate will see through this motu proprio and
distance himself from it. They will have to be
discreet but they will do so. My own bishop has
been very quick to point out that he sees no need
to change anything. We have fought for the Mass
before and we must do it again. It is not a time
for despondency but a time for action and rolling
up sleeves to defeat this latest liturgical assassin.

We need to take time to find out more about what it was
like, what a long journey it's been. Among other crucial
documents, I recommend reading Alfred Marnau's "The
1971 'English' Indult—a Recollection";[1] "An Exhorta-
tion Against Discouragement, by My Father" by Gregory
DiPippo;[2] "Resistance is Never Futile: An Interview with

---

1   Available at https://lms.org.uk/1971-english-indult-recollection.
2   Published at *New Liturgical Movement* on July 24, 2021: https://
www.newliturgicalmovement.org/2021/07/an-exhortation-against-
discouragement.html.

Christian Marquant, founder of Paix Liturgique,"[3] which tells about the early days of the French traditionalist movement, including exciting moments of lay uprisings and church seizures;[4] Leo Darroch's *Una Voce: The History of the Foederatio Internationalis Una Voce*, which amply illustrates the incomprehension, obstructionism, animosity, and double-dealing to which the lovers of tradition were subjected every step of the way;[5] and, most of all, the short history you are holding in your hands. The more we read about this heroic generation and the obstacles they overcame, the more inspired we will be to do in our day what they did in theirs. Our forerunners in the movement are sources of hope, courage, and guidance for us today. How harrowing the stories of what ordinary Catholics had to do and suffer just to attend a Latin Mass *once in a while*! They persevered against monumental odds that might remind one of the great battle scenes in *The Lord of the Rings*, about which any "rational analysis" would have concluded: Sauron will triumph.

It is no different today in 2021. We must do as our forefathers in the traditional movement did, and be cowed by no one's threats, dissuaded by no one's animosity, deterred by no obstacle, seduced by no "good enough" or "tolerable" alternative.

One thing we must keep front and center before our eyes: what we are fighting for is good, sacred, Catholic, and worthy of our deepest devotion. It cannot be all of

---

3 Published at *Rorate Caeli* on December 16, 2020: https://rorate-caeli.blogspot.com/2020/12/resistance-is-never-futile-interview.html.
4 See also my article, "French traditionalists show us how to take back our churches when closed by bishops," *LifeSiteNews*, November 24, 2020: https://www.lifesitenews.com/blogs/french-traditionalists-show-us-how-to-take-back-our-churches-when-closed-by-bishops/.
5 See Appendix II for a discussion of Darroch's book.

a sudden forbidden or declared dangerous. And we are not disobedient for holding fast to it or seeking it. The traditional movement would not exist at all if, at the beginning of the final phase of "liturgical reform," Catholics had not persistently gone against the wishes and even the legal determinations of Paul VI and other bishops. Paul VI began to relent just a little; John Paul II acknowledged the rightfulness of the traditionalists' aspirations; and then Benedict XVI opened up the treasury to everyone. The legitimacy of that initial "disobedience" was eventually accepted. The traditionalists had in fact fought on the basis of true principles and for true goods that the Church needs and will always need.

We are under siege again, from a pope who has proved implacably hostile to any other way of living Catholicism than his one-world progressive humanistic interreligious all-are-welcome corporation. The icy wind of official disfavor is blowing against us after decades of gradual thaw under John Paul II and Benedict XVI.

This time around, however, there are very many more of us—millions of laity and thousands of TLM-loving priests and religious across the globe. We occupy positions within seminaries and chanceries. In certain cases, we have good rapport and even influence with bishops who appreciate our fidelity, zeal, intelligence, and love for Christ and His Church. We have cornered the market on scholarship and intellectual credibility: for any one book written by a progressive, there are ten better ones written by conservatives or traditionalists. In the Church, at least, the liberal agenda is tired, ageing, and lashing out with the spasms of an animal *in extremis*.

If Pope Francis and his allies really believe they can tear the love of sacred tradition out of the hearts of Catholic clergy, religious, and laity simply by a papal pronunciamento and a sinister scowl, they are more to be pitied for their delusionality than blamed for their malice. In point of fact, the more they try, the more incandescent this love will glow. They will not be able to win this battle of attrition. As we have seen, many bishops understand the way things are on the ground and, from enlightened self-interest if not always from sympathy, are prepared to keep the peace with traditionalists.

The post-*Traditionis* world will still be a battlefield. It will flare up here and there into intense conflict. Some priests will be suspended, stripped of faculties, transferred to Siberia. Among these, some will go independent and others will go underground, saying Mass in living rooms or open fields. Large, flourishing parish communities may get the ungracious axe. Good bishops who prudently dispensed from the onerous provisions of *Traditionis* may, upon forced or canonical retirement, be replaced by Bergoglian clones. Most terrifying of all, prospering religious communities and societies of apostolic life may find themselves hounded, denounced, burdened with commissioners, coerced into changing their constitutions. Neither hard-liners nor the cooperative will have an easy escape: the former will risk being scattered to the four winds, the latter being subdued into puppets of the regime. Again, I am not saying that this *will* happen everywhere and to everyone, but that it *could* happen to anyone, anywhere. Miracles of deliverance will be needed and prayed for.

For several *centuries*, Christians in the early Church were persecuted and then tolerated, persecuted and tolerated, by successive Roman Emperors. One could never be quite sure what the next emperor would bring. We can also think of the Catholics in England at the time of the Reformation. Within a period of decades the country went from a regime hostile to Catholics to a respite under

Queen Mary, only to be thrust again into the Protestant Elizabeth's reign, under whom so many martyrs shed their blood. Alas, the papacy too has become politicized in the manner of a country staggering back and forth between rival political parties. Benedict's reign was followed by Francis's, and we know not what the future holds. Things could get very much worse. The essential task of the Christian remains ever the same: to believe in, to follow, and to bear witness to Christ, even at the cost of life.

Our greatest danger lies in our having become *soft*. Generally speaking, the lives of modern Western people are easy, comfortable, and convenient, with suffering excluded wherever and whenever possible. We are surrounded by mesmerizing and entertaining technology that lulls us to contentment. We have a thousand reasons and ways to put off "extra" work, "needless" suffering, and "inconvenient" impositions.

More specifically, many young traditionalists today were born with silver spoons in their mouths, so to speak— into a parish run by the Priestly Fraternity of St. Peter or the Institute of Christ the King Sovereign Priest, or into a diocese where clergy had brought the TLM into their parishes. In parts of the world where bishops implemented *Summorum Pontificum* or at least refrained from blocking it, we've enjoyed the availability of Masses in multiple locations, perhaps within easy driving distance. Sometimes we can choose between a High Mass here and a Solemn Mass over there. In such areas, Catholics have come to enjoy, and to count on, plentiful access to Catholic tradition.

Those of us who have never had to "fight for the rite" may not *yet* be the tough men our forefathers, who persevered in the midst of hopeless conditions, had to be. They did not let threatened penalties or tempting blandishments ("oh sure, we'll set up an *ad orientem* Latin Novus Ordo for you once a month!") deter them—and neither should we. If we are a bit soft, *Traditionis Custodes* was our heaven-sent wakeup call. "When I was a child, I spoke as a child, I understood as a child, I thought as a child. But when I became a man, I put away the things of a child" (1 Cor. 13:11). In a period of peace, there are gentler ways to mature; but we do not choose the times we live in, and Divine Providence chose us for *this* time. As a Carmelite priest wrote to me: "It can give us courage to remember that God, from all eternity, has willed and chosen that we live in and through this evil age, so that we faithfully hold on to the light of the Faith and pass on the torch amidst this unprecedented darkness, for our own sanctification and salvation and that of the next generation. Such times form saints of those who are generous and persevering in the divine service."

Most of us will not have the privilege of shedding our blood for Christ. In the present age of the Church, many are now being called to a dry or white martyrdom for the sake of her glorious Tradition, shamefully marginalized by those who should most cherish and protect it. Now is not the time to ask: "Is it worth the trouble?" *Rorate Caeli* tweeted on July 25: "Each Sunday you are able to go to a Latin Mass is not only an infinite Blessing from above—it's also, in human terms, a counterrevolutionary & countercultural act all wrapped into one. You're not supposed to be there—which is why more than ever you *are* supposed to be there."

We should resist the well-meaning but treacherous advice: "Just give up on the fight; don't make an idol of the Mass..." This implies that whenever we love some-thing enough to live for it, to fight and die for it, we are making it an idol—as if only God could deserve such

total commitment. This is false. Although God alone is
to be adored, that does not mean He alone deserves our
commitment. We should be ready to die for our spouse,
child, or neighbor; for the good of virtue; for the sake
of the truth; for our country. We should be ready to live
and die for the Mass or any sacrament or any dogma of
the Faith. We should have this disposition because these
things, although not God, are from Him and for Him,
uniting us to Him the way a photo or a letter unites us
to someone beloved, or the way a face unites us to the
heart of the person who shines through the face. If we do
not understand this point, we will soon be condemning
marriage and religious vows, as some heretics did in search
of a "pure love of God." We are not a sect of Buddhists
who seek to escape from flesh-and-blood realities, but
Catholics who see the world sacramentally.

The battle over tradition is a battle over *realities*, not
ideas or opinions or preferences. We have a weighty *respon-
sibility* for these created goods; Our Lord assures us that
our final judgment depends, to a large extent, on what
we have done with and to one another, *and* how we have
invested the valuable "talents" (in ancient times, a huge
quantity of money) entrusted to us. Nor should we pay
heed to those who accuse us of lacking humility because of
our ecclesial stance. Part of humility is clinging to the truth
without embarrassment or second-guessing, acknowledging
it as a gift that we have received through no merit of our
own, and then treating it not like a private possession but
as a common good meant to be shared: we recognize not
only that what was sacred and great remains so today,
but that *all Catholics ought to know it*—it is a good that
benefits everyone, near and far, now and always.

They may take away our buildings, but they cannot
take away the faith that built them and can build them

anew. They may temporarily take from us the Mass of
the Ages, but they cannot extinguish the love of the Mass
that will outlast our enemies' hatred. They can violate
our rights as sons of the Church, but they cannot cancel
out our supernatural dignity as sons of God. They can
strip us of human recourse, but they cannot block our
recourse to the Holy Mother of God and all the saints
who worship the Lamb upon His throne, and who will
always intercede for those who love Tradition as they did.
Let us never lose heart as we move from a time of rela-
tive peace to a time of secret struggles and open conflict,
armed by Christ with "the armor of God, that [we] may
be able to resist in the evil day, and to stand in all things
perfect... [our] loins girt about with truth, and having on
the breastplate of justice... In all things taking the shield
of faith . . . the helmet of salvation, and the sword of the
Spirit" (Eph. 6:11–17).

Peter A. Kwasniewski
Feast of the Triumph of the Holy Cross
September 14, 2021

Preface

TO THE ANGELICO EDITION

W HEN I WROTE THE INTRODUCTION (below) to a projected series of articles beginning in 2012, my focus was on explaining to a new generation of traditionalist Catholics the origins of the movement, its initial trials and struggles, and its eventual vindication by *Summorum Pontificum*. I felt obliged to adopt an almost apologetic tone in setting forth this history, for had not Pope Benedict expressed the wish that we put aside the conflicts and grudges of the past and seek to work together for the benefit of the Church? I hardly thought that nine years later Pope Francis would explicitly reject Pope Benedict's initiative and attempt to resurrect for Catholic traditionalists the darkest days of confrontation and persecution—although from the very first days of his papacy that had been a menacing possibility. So my little volume is no longer merely the reminder of a bitter yet heroic past, forgetful as we Americans tend to be of our heritage. Now it may serve as a guide and handbook for the trials that will be coming to us, in greater or lesser measure. For to know our history is the best armament in confronting the future.

The contents of this book appeared over the years as posts on the blog of the Society of St. Hugh of Cluny, an organization which since 2007 has promoted the celebration of the traditional liturgy and the recovery of the Catholic artistic and musical heritage. The chapters fall naturally into two clusters. The first covers the genesis and development of the traditionalist movement up to Pope Francis's reign. The second is a more detailed account of events from 2020 onwards, leading up to *Traditionis Custodes*. I have left these remarks in the form in which they were first written for the weblog of the Society of St. Hugh of Cluny. The texts have been lightly edited for their inclusion herein, but no attempt has been made to revise each chapter in light of subsequent events (such as *Traditionis Custodes*), as it was thought better to leave their original style as photographic snapshots of a movement in motion.

My thanks to Peter Kwasniewski for his tireless initiative in getting this publication off the ground, his editing work, and his eloquent Foreword. I would also like to thank my wife Jill who edited the manuscript (do we even have such a thing anymore?) and has provided her usual sagacious suggestions.

Introduction

SINCE THE PROMULGATION OF *SUMMO-rum Pontificum* in 2007, the Catholic traditionalist movement has exited the ecclesiastical "skid row" (Prof. Robert Spaemann) and has been entering, tentatively and with some setbacks, the Catholic mainstream. Even some of the "crown jewels" of the Church in the Northeast United States have seen at least one traditional Mass: e.g., St. Mary's in New Haven, Connecticut (near Yale University); St. Patrick's Cathedral, New York; University Church at Fordham University, New York; the upper Church of the Basilica of the National Shrine of the Immaculate Conception in Washington, D.C. And, at least in the greater New York area, Solemn High Masses are regularly celebrated on major feasts—in one or two locations, even every Sunday.

This liturgical renaissance has attracted an ever-growing following of the young and religiously committed and their growing families. At traditional Masses nowadays the average congregation is often substantially younger than that of the "ordinary form" Novus Ordo services.

These new converts to Catholic Tradition often wonder: how did this come about? How did the traditional liturgy disappear, who kept it alive in deed and memory during the intervening years, and how was it revived? At a conference in September 2011 sponsored by the Society of St. Hugh of Cluny, Prof. Luc Perrin of the University of Strasbourg presented a short history of French traditionalism. A reader on the French site *Forum*

1

Catholique asked if an equivalent essay existed for the US. In response, I offer the following sketch as an attempt to give some answers and to point out lines of inquiry for the historians of the future.

The reader should take these notes as the personal reflections of an observer. I disclaim any inside knowledge and recognize that this essay, given my lack of access to the documentation, can only be a preliminary undertaking. The reader will also note an emphasis on events on the East Coast of the United States—that's where my own experiences are concentrated.

I have structured this work on the development of traditionalism after Vatican II roughly according to decades— although this is no more than a handy convention to impose order on a chaotic flow of events. For example, if I call the period 1975–1985 "The Era of Conservative Catholicism," I am well aware that the genesis of this school of thought dates back to the late 1960s and new manifestations continue to appear right to the present day.

I ask the reader's indulgence on an additional matter. In the "era of good feeling" after *Summorum Pontificum*, Catholics—traditionalists, conservatives, and the Church establishment—were enjoined to cultivate mutual respect, supposedly leading to "mutual enrichment." One must, however, speak honestly. I cannot avoid setting forth the sins of the clergy any I more than I can conceal the limitations both of those who struggled so valiantly in the traditionalist cause and of their "conservative Catholic" contemporaries. And now, of course, under Pope Francis, at least the Church establishment and the Vatican have adopted an entirely different attitude towards conflict within the Church.

Finally, I limit myself to the broad outlines and the main movements with which I am familiar. Certain

"traditionalist" or quasi-traditionalist movements and individuals, such as the "sedevacantists," or the independent
priests, are covered only in passing or not mentioned at
all because (a) they remained tangential to the traditionalist mainstream; and (b) I have very little information
to provide on their activities.

1 *The Birth of Traditionalism*

TRIUMPH, 1965–1975

T HE SECOND VATICAN COUNCIL AND ITS
implementing decrees hit the American Church
like a tidal wave. Catholics today cannot realize—or have forgotten—how sudden the changes were:
the abandonment of Latin, the reorientation of the altars,
the introduction of Protestant hymns and "folk music."
And all this was years before the advent of the Novus
Ordo in 1969. At the same time, a chorus of voices within
the Church arose that challenged the basics of Christian
morality, the rules of the religious orders, and the hierarchy
of the Church. These intellectual movements quickly took
on physical form: the fasting rules were relaxed and then
virtually abandoned; churches were gutted and renovated
across the country; nuns progressively simplified their
habits and then most ditched them altogether. The first
signs of disintegration in the priesthood, religious orders,
and schools appeared.

Certainly, in this country there was little understanding among the mass of the laity of these changes. Yet
at the same time there was virtually no resistance. The
"renewal" had been ordered by authority; that was the end
of the story for most American Catholics. There was no
American equivalent of the Don Camillo tale in which

5

the congregation—led by the village communist—rises up to block the introduction of a new saint by a visiting priest. Indeed, the really interesting aspect of the American traditionalist movement in the first years after the Council was that there wasn't any. The wave of "renewal" rolled on without confronting organized opposition. Those isolated souls who expressed disagreement with one or another change on whatever grounds—or who just sought an explanation of what was going on—were confronted and quickly suppressed. The implementers of the Council pursuant to "The Spirit of Vatican II" were not disposed to justify their actions to anyone.

There were exceptions to the general conformity. Scurrilous poems circulated in the pews lampooning the *Novus Ordo*. On a more serious note, in 1965, even while the Council was drawing to an end, Father Gommar de Pauw (a distinguished priest originally from Belgium) announced his opposition to the *Novus Ordo*—and maintained his loyalty to the Old Mass and its public practice throughout the years to come. He founded the Catholic Traditionalist Movement and later, in 1968 Ave Maria chapel on Long Island, where the traditional rite continues to be celebrated up to the present day. Fr. De Pauw also launched and continued for many years an energetic publicity campaign in defense of Tradition.[1] He was the best-known representative of "independent priests" who did likewise.

We might also cite in this context John Senior, who co-founded the "Integrated Humanities Program" at the University of Kansas in 1970. It flourished until the university authorities took care to shut it down. It is characteristic of those years that this, the most influential institutional initiative of the early traditionalist movement (John Senior later allied himself with the FSSPX) concerned itself

---

[1] https://en.wikipedia.org/wiki/Gommar_DePauw.

directly with the teaching of literature and philosophy, not liturgy, at a secular university![2]

But the most significant American resistance to the Conciliar innovations in those years was intellectual and theoretical, rather than practical or organizational. In September 1967, Dietrich von Hildebrand, Thomas Molnar, and John A. McManemin joined in founding a United States chapter of *Una Voce*. Von Hildebrand and Molnar were among the first contributors to *Triumph* magazine (see below), while McManemin was active in the development of Catholic liturgical music. Like Fr. De Pauw, Molnar and von Hildebrand were Europeans by birth and education. The new organization, contemporary press reports emphasized, was composed of laymen—which became a defining traditionalist characteristic. It protested from the start the progressive elimination of Latin from the liturgy. *Una Voce* US seems to have held meetings until about 1970. Perhaps the most lasting legacy of the US chapter of *Una Voce* was a memorable and prophetic statement of principle delivered by the head of the international *Una Voce* federation, Eric de Saventhem, at a meeting of the US chapter in 1970:

> A renaissance will come: asceticism and adoration as the mainspring of direct total dedication to Christ will return. Confraternities of priests, vowed to celibacy and to an intense life of prayer and meditation will be formed. Religious will regroup themselves into houses of "strict observance." A new form of "Liturgical Movement" will come into being, led by young priests and attracting young people, in protest against the flat, prosaic, philistine or delirious liturgies which

---

2 See, generally, Fr. Francis Bethel, OSB, *John Senior and the Restoration of Realism* (Merrimack, NH: Thomas More College Press, 2016).

will soon overgrow and finally smother even the
recently revised rites...

It is important that these new priests and
religious, these new young people with ardent
hearts, should find—if only in a corner of the
rambling mansion of the Church—the treasure
of a true sacred liturgy...

This, before Archbishop Marcel Lefebvre had really begun
to organize in Europe! Regrettably, *Una Voce* US seems to
have ceased operations shortly after this stirring speech
was given.[3]

These early traditionalists gave us some important books
attacking the theological and philosophical foundations
of Catholic progressivism. We think of Thomas Molnar's
Ecumenism or New Reformation? (also known as *Dialogues
and Ideologues*)[4] and of Dietrich von Hildebrand's *Trojan
Horse in the City of God.*[5] These works had an impact outside the United States—in von Hildebrand's case, a to-be-
expected hostile reception among German Church circles.
Molnar later contributed an early—and coming from the
conservative spectrum, perhaps unprecedented—critical
assessment of Pope Paul VI in *The Counter-Revolution.*[6]

L. Brent Bozell launched *Triumph* magazine in 1966.
Its origins dated back to the divergence of views, developing since the early 1960s, between Bozell and William
F. Buckley at *National Review*—thus, even before the
Council. Bozell and his allies were concerned about the
drift of American conservatism to uncritical support of
capitalism and the "American Way." They revolted against

3 Leo Darroch, *Una Voce: The History of the Foederatio Internationalis Una Voce 1964–2003* (Leominster, UK: Gracewing, 2017),
at 19–22.
4 First edition, New York: Funk & Wagnalls, 1968.
5 First edition, Chicago: Franciscan Herald Press, 1967.
6 New York: Funk & Wagnalls, 1969, at 164–78.

American conservatism's abandonment of the struggle against the social and intellectual pathologies of modernity in an attempt to form a common front against communism and to uphold liberal (in the original sense of the word) democracy and economics. These conflicts gave rise to a community among conservative Catholic scholars, writers, and journalists. Prof. Perrin has emphasized the critical role of existing "networks" in France growing out of preconciliar political and ecclesiastical struggles as providing the foundation for the traditionalist resistance in that country. In just this one instance, a similar grouping also existed in the US.[7]

To undertake the struggle against modernity, Bozell assembled for *Triumph* a rare group of writers—some of whom we have previously encountered: Thomas Molnar, Frederick Wilhelmsen, Dietrich von Hildebrand, Warren Carroll, Gary Potter and many others. *Triumph* embarked upon a searching critique of developments within the Church while always remaining aware of the interaction of the ecclesiastical realm with politics, society, culture, and the economy. Uncompromisingly (and at that time, thanklessly) orthodox, its very name challenged Catholic progressivism, with its hatred of the "triumphalist" Church of yore.[8]

The insights this magazine offered were endless. *Triumph* rightly predicted that the conservatism of *National Review* would end in a variant of the "liberalism" it had

---

7 On *Triumph* and its founder, see Mark D. Popowski, *The Rise and Fall of* Triumph: *The History of a Radical Roman Catholic Magazine, 1966–76* (Lanham, MD: Lexington Books, 2012); Daniel Kelly, *Living on Fire: The Life of L. Brent Bozell Jr.* (Wilmington, DE: ISI Books, 2014).

8 Christopher Derrick, "In Defense of Triumphalism," May 1970, in *The Best of* Triumph (Front Royal, VA: Christendom Press, 2001), 123.

been created to oppose. Before the terms "neoconservative" and "paleoconservative" existed, Bozell and company dared suggest that the so-called American experiment could be deeply, inherently flawed. And years before *Roe v. Wade* the editors not only wrote against abortion but conducted the first direct actions against the abortion industry.[9]

In its very first year *Triumph* argued for the preservation of Latin in the Catholic liturgy.[10] *Triumph* was the first—40 years before Alcuin Read—to expose the doings of a "liturgy club" of insiders in demolishing Catholic worship.[11] Needless to say, *Triumph* offered the first detailed critique of the Novus Ordo upon its appearance. (It published a special twelve-page supplement on the "Ottaviani Intervention" in 1969.[12])

But the most obvious observation we can make regarding the *Triumph* generation of writers—as basic as it may seem—was that *they were right*. At a time when the entire official Catholic world was either celebrating the achievements of the Council or pushing for further radical change, *Triumph* revealed the dark aspects, warned of the developing catastrophe. It is the analysis of the contributors to *Triumph*—not that of the clerical establishment and its in-house press—that has subsequently proven to accord with reality.

---

9   "Action for Life," July 1970, in *The Best of* Triumph, 19.

10   Dietrich von Hildebrand, "The Case for the Latin Mass," October 1966, in *The Best of* Triumph, 62. Also reprinted in *The Charitable Anathema*. (The "Latin Mass" in this case simply means not doing the old Mass in the vernacular, as was already happening from about 1965 onwards. We are still a few years out from the imposition of the Novus Ordo.)

11   Gary K. Potter, "The Liturgy Club," May 1, 1968, in *The Best of* Triumph, 77.

12   https://remnantnewspaper.com/web/index.php/articles/item/3068-the-remnant-in-1969-holy-father-do-not-destroy-the-mass.

Not all of their judgments, however, were equally sound. *Triumph* celebrated the publication of *Humanae Vitae* as a glorious turning point for the Church, as the vindication of papal authority after the postconciliar chaos. Now, said the editors, it was time to rally around Pope Paul and join the counterattack that he had initiated.[13] In this they were grievously mistaken. They had declared the war over when the struggle had just begun—as the liturgical revolution took off, as the transformation of the "American Catholic Church" from passive conformism to active progressivism gained momentum with the foreknowledge and at the direction of the Vatican (e.g., the episcopal appointments engineered by Archbishop Jadot). *Triumph*'s newfound uncritical enthusiasm for the Vatican stood in all too obvious conflict with the facts recorded in its own pages. I have always believed that this inherent contradiction—just as much as financial difficulties and the tragic health problems of its editor-in-chief—led to the publication's untimely demise in 1975.[14]

So, *Triumph* disappeared. To this day no traditionalist successor publication has surpassed it in depth, sophistication, and intellectual courage. And none has enjoyed the same universal recognition in American traditionalism. Yet, Bozell and his team had not labored in vain. The seeds of an eventual revival were planted in the minds of both the surviving contributors and their former and future readers.

One afternoon, years later, my studies in the library of a prominent non-Catholic law school were interrupted by a shattering crash. A distinguished professor of law, getting on in years and at the point of retirement, had

---

13   E.g., "*Habemus Papam*," August 1968, in *The Best of* Triumph, 101.

14   Several newsletters and a collection of articles appeared through the middle of 1976: see Kelly, *Living on Fire*, 183–84.

fallen at his desk. As I helped him to his feet, I noted that the professor—whom I had not even suspected of being Catholic at all—had been engaged in carefully cataloguing his precious back issues of *Triumph*. We looked at each other and smiled...

2 The Heyday of "Conservative Catholicism"

1975–1985

THE FORCES OF TRADITION IN THE CATH-
olic Church of the United States appeared
routed by 1975. No support had been found
in the Church establishment. Very few practical alternatives
to the tidal wave of conciliar reform had ever been offered;
and the mouthpiece of the resistance movement, *Triumph*,
had folded ignominiously. Yet it was at this moment that
a new rival to the forces of the establishment took on
definite form. It was the start of the flowering of "conservative Catholicism."

Now the movement dates back well before 1975. We
could cite the split in the Matt family between the "factions" of *The Wanderer* (conservative) and *The Remnant* (traditionalist) in 1967. The reaction of Brent Bozell and the
editors of *Triumph* to *Humanae Vitae* in 1968 could serve
as another point of departure. And, speaking of Bozell,
his—preconciliar!—estrangement from Bill Buckley and
the *National Review* party line already illustrated fundamental differences between "traditional" and "conservative"
Catholicism. Similarly, new manifestations of "conservative
Catholicism" continued to appear well after 1985—indeed,

First Things, its most representative forum, dates from 1990. Yet it was in the second postconciliar decade that the conservative Catholics became a coherent force with the appearance of their key institutions and leaders.

In contrast to traditionalism, conservative Catholics "accepted" unconditionally the Council and the new Mass (at least initially!). Entirely consistently, they also adopted as their own the "modern world" and specifically the "American Experiment." Yet at the same time they did not have many good things to say about the actual government of the American polity nor (at least at this early stage), the state or leadership of the Church in the United States as well. Indeed, they readily acknowledged the deep crisis in which the Church found herself.

How could the conservatives explain this unhappy situation? It was the fault, they said, of "dissident" forces within the Church: liberals and radicals who had rejected that papal authority which still provided a sure guiding light and to which conservatives always appealed—both in theory and often in actual practice (e.g., petitions to the nuncio in Washington!). The crisis of the Church was in essence a crisis of obedience (as formulated by Msgr. George Kelly). Regardless of whatever else was being done or said, following blindly the Pope and the Vatican was the only course to take in a time of confusion.

Now in fact the positions of conservative Catholics were very diverse, reflecting the absence of any central doctrine or authority. While some restricted their unconditional loyalty to the papacy alone and critiqued and even confronted "dissenting" prelates, others (like the organization "Catholics United for the Faith") proclaimed a duty of blind obedience to all bishops or even to all priests. Some celebrated what they considered the continuing successes of the Church establishment, while others, like *The Wanderer*, were so severe in their criticism of the "American Catholic Church" as to be at times barely distinguishable from the traditionalist untouchables. Figures like Fr. Bruce Ritter of Covenant House fame were proclaimed "conservatives" simply for opposing abortion or pornography (a view of course shared by the secular news media).

The political and economic positions of the conservatives were likewise hardly monolithic. Most, however, forcefully defended American capitalism against "liberal" and socialist critics. Most took a firm anti-communist stance, whether confronting the continuing threat of the Soviet Union (and opposing, for example, the American Church's flirtation with disarmament) or pro-socialist tendencies in the Catholic Church itself (like liberation theology). Above all, they concentrated on "life issues": preeminently, opposition to abortion.

As the 70s and 80s progressed the religious conservatives started to acquire their own literature (e.g., Msgr. George A. Kelly's *The Battle for the American Church*[1]) and leaders (George Weigel and Richard John Neuhaus among many others). They established new colleges like Thomas Aquinas or Christendom (the latter an offshoot of a *Triumph* magazine program!). New magazines came into being: *Human Life Review* (1975), *Crisis in Catholicism* (1982), *First Things* (1990)—in addition to already existing conservative-friendly publications like *National Review, Homiletic and Pastoral Review,* or *The Wanderer.* And there was of course a plethora of new organizations, including the Catholic League for Religious and Civil Rights, the aforementioned Catholics United for the Faith, Human Life International and many more—often sporting Latin names (*Regnum Christi*). Some of the creations of this era, like Ignatius Press or EWTN, were truly amazing

---

1   Garden City, NY: Image Books, 1981.

accomplishments—especially when one considers how
their founders had to face the hierarchy's indifference and
often active opposition.

On the liturgical front, the conservatives accepted the
Novus Ordo as an article of faith. They could not, however,
ignore the massive liturgical abuses which showed no sign
of abating. In this early period the conservatives' "hermeneutic" was *strict construction* of the Novus Ordo liturgical
texts. According to the conservatives, careful examination
of the liturgical legislation revealed that many abuses had
no foundation, while other practices that had been pro-
scribed (like use of the Latin language, Gregorian chant,
or celebration *ad orientem*) were specifically allowed. It was
on this basis that the Latin Liturgy Association (dedicated
to the use of Latin in the Novus Ordo, in contrast to the
similarly named Latin Mass Society in the UK) started
from 1975 promoting the return of Latin to the liturgy.

As a result of these initiatives, at least the Latin language returned to the liturgy, even if mostly at irregular
intervals and in out-of-the-way locations (like, in the early
1980s, the former Lithuanian parish of Our Lady of Vilna
in New York City). In these services Catholics struggled
to incorporate the Church's liturgical and artistic heritage
into the Novus Ordo and to purge it of abuses. As the
movement advanced, even regular parishes offering Latin
Novus Ordo Masses were established in at least one or
two locations (like St. Agnes in St. Paul, Minnesota led
by Msgr. Richard J. Schuler since 1969).

Experience soon revealed the limitations of these
endeavors. The establishment remained indifferent to the
would-be restorers of the liturgy. The inherent flexibility of
the Novus Ordo meant that a significant degree of unpre-
dictability was an ineradicable feature of all these "Latin
language" liturgies. There was no universally accepted point

of reference for the ceremony or music for celebrating the Novus Ordo in Latin—like that provided by the Oratory in the UK. Eccentricity all too often prevailed among the celebrants, congregations, and sponsoring organizations. At one such "Latin Mass" in Princeton, New Jersey, the priest decided to give the sermon in Latin!

What was the result of these efforts? The conservatives helped a whole new generation of Catholics to rediscover something of the theological, liturgical, and moral heritage of the Church. Their critiques put into words what many younger Catholics were experiencing with unease. Many important social and ecclesiastical initiatives were launched, and many political battles were engaged. For example, it was increasingly to the credit of the conservatives that the Catholic Church remained a critical player in the prolife cause—after the hierarchy had gotten cold feet, having realized that this issue was driving a wedge between them and the power elite of American civil society. The conservatives had put the spotlight on certain abuses—like child abuse and the "lavender mafia"—decades before the secular press had perceived anything was amiss. Yet the failings and missed opportunities were at least as great.

First, from the middle of the 1980s the leadership of conservative organizations and associations showed an alarming tendency to self-destruct either morally, theologically, or both. An early example was the above mentioned Covenant House. This was a serious liability, given that the usual organizational form of these groups was absolute rule of a charismatic, authoritarian individual.

Second, except for a minority of individual priests, bishops, and small, unrepresentative religious orders, conservatives acquired no following in the institutional Church in the United States. Indeed, they aroused berserk rage to the extent they publicly criticized prelates, attempted

to go over the heads of certain bishops to nuncios or the
Vatican, or just declined to join in the official Catholic
press's hosannas to the establishment. Archbishop Weakland's memoirs offer eloquent testimony of this. The only
critical commentary acceptable to the hierarchy was that
emanating from a Catholic left having political, social, and
media connections the bishops both feared and secretly
envied. It was tragic that the Catholic conservatives, the
would-be "party of the establishment," were in fact themselves the "dissenters"!

Third, the conservatives' conviction that at least the
Vatican was on their side was delusional. Would the Vatican
discipline the very prelates it had appointed—usually with
the advice or at the instigation of the existing episcopal
team? At most John Paul II imposed a limited outward
conformity. While isolated elements of the conservatives'
rhetoric might be welcome now and then in Rome, in
no way did the Vatican support any kind of systematic
renewal or restoration in the conservative sense. Usually
the gentlemen in the Vatican understood their real role
as navigating between various incompatible individuals,
forces, and trends without making any attempt to initiate
reform. The conservatives might vaunt the orthodoxy of
their newly-founded colleges, but at all times the Vatican
set greater store on Notre Dame University than Thomas
Aquinas College—and Harvard was more important to
them than either! For both good and bad reasons, the
conservatives' economic and political ideas had even less
resonance in Rome.

For example, with the election of the "Polish Pope,"
John Paul II, in 1978 it seemed the Church had finally
acquired a leader to the conservatives' taste. Certainly,
John Paul II's participation in the events leading up to
the collapse of the Soviet empire in 1989–91 fulfilled the

wildest dreams of the conservatives regarding the Church's role in politics. But as a governor of the Church, John Paul had an entirely different impact. Despite all the activity of the conservatives, their "dissenting" foes in the hierarchy and the religious orders remained untouched and in good standing. It was the same in the matter of new appointments: for every O'Connor or Law appointed by John Paul II there was a Bernardin or Mahony.

Finally, a related and more significant, if subtle, problem was inherent in the devotion of Catholic conservatism to the principle of authority. It might seem the conservatives were hardheaded realists. Yet despite their often unsparing criticism of the state of the Church and their relentless activity in so many apostolates, at the end of the day they secretly cherished the conviction that, at least at the very top level, all was well with the Church. They took it as axiomatic that at least the Pope had a plan and they could wait for him and his bishops to implement it—assisting when needed. A pervasive sense of complacency was the inevitable result. Problems continued to be ignored and arbitrary assumptions and wishful thinking substituted for facts. Meanwhile the destruction of the Church at every level proceeded.

We may ask ourselves at this point how the conservatives differed from the phenomenon of what were later called "movements": organizations, often of a mixed lay and clerical character, which departed in significant respects from the traditional Catholic paradigm of the religious order. Indeed, in these years there arose in the US at least one such "movement"—*Miles Jesu*—that might be assigned to the conservative camp. Yet the differences between the conservative Catholics and the movement community remained great. First, while the conservatives were, on the whole, economic and social conservatives as well, that could be said of only a minority of the movements. Second, while the conservatives, certainly in this period, pursued a policy of open criticism of the American Church, the movements had from the beginning made cultivating the favor of the hierarchy a key element of their plans. Third, there seems to be some instinctive lack of resonance of the "movement" concept in American conservatism. In the early 80s, *Opus Dei* organized at least one public conference in New York featuring conservative greats but as far as I am aware never repeated this initiative. The Legion of Christ—a priestly congregation rather than a lay "movement"—stood aloof. It was only much later that it tried through its lay arm *Regnum Christi* to organize conservative lay forces (like homeschoolers) for its own benefit. Other movements, like Communion and Liberation or the Neocatechumenal Way, may have had strong ties to some members of the hierarchy but didn't have a meaningful presence in the US. The result was that no one organization was able to give overall direction and focus to the conservative efforts.

Now what of the "traditionalists"?

It was around this time (1973) that a branch of the FSSPX—the Priestly Fraternity of St. Pius X—was set up in the United States, just a few years after the start of Archbishop Lefebvre's seminary in Switzerland. It was a revolutionary act: a group of traditional Catholics acknowledged that the crisis of the Church had assumed such a magnitude that action even independent of the hierarchy and the Vatican was justified. This meant not just celebrating the traditional Mass, but organizing seminaries, schools, chapels, religious orders and monasteries both purely traditional and independent of the institutional Church. It was, in retrospect, an amazing step. Perhaps, in the American context, its greatest significance lies in the concept of a state of emergency. Among all the Catholic factions—liberal, conservative, or progressive—only the FSSPX had a real sense of urgency, the instinct that catastrophe loomed unless action were taken.

In retrospect, this was a justifiable, even necessary course of action—yet in practical terms the impact of the FSSPX in the United States was limited. In a way it was absurd to expect such an ecclesiastical "civil disobedience" movement to flourish in a country that was the very heartland of blind obedience to the clergy. But there were also early crises of the Fraternity that couldn't just be ascribed to the uniquely inhospitable environment of the United States. For example, the departure of nine priests in 1983 to form the sedevacantist Society of Pius V—and later the founding of other sedevacantist groups—revealed unresolved differences of opinion within the FSSPX.

Despite these struggles, the FSSPX continued to steadily grow over the years, adding new chapels, seminaries, and schools. What it could not do, however, was act as any kind of general rallying point for traditionalists in the United States—just as the none of the established "movements" could do the same for the conservatives. While its European parent almost immediately created a critical challenge for both the French Church and the Vatican, the American branch of the FSSPX could be safely ignored by the American hierarchy.

And what of the other traditionalists—the "Uniate" ones?

These years were indeed the "winter of (their) discontent." Aside from the liturgies of a few individual priests, no official traditional Masses were celebrated. Publications like *The Remnant* helped showcase contributions originating mainly from Europe (Michael Davies, for example). Groups in the New York area like the *Roman Forum* helped keep the cause alive by sponsoring lectures and symposia. In addition to European visitors, contributors to these events included *Triumph* veterans and some new faces (like John Rao). It was at this time that *Una Voce* reorganized on these shores—it contributed initially more talk and little else. Yet all these activities helped maintain awareness of what was happening elsewhere in the world and kept the seemingly absurd hope alive that the traditional cause one day would be restored. It was a struggle for survival.

It was in this closed, asphyxiating environment that the letter *Quattuor Abhinc Annos* (3 October 1984) and even more so the motu proprio *Ecclesia Dei* (2 July 1988) hit like bombshells. The "Indult" regime, authorizing the celebration of the traditional Mass, was born. It was an extraordinary change—something both the Catholic establishment and the conservative Catholics had said was impossible. Yet American traditionalists had had precious little to do with bringing it about. It was a victory attributable to the efforts of other men in other countries.

3 Return from the Catacombs

THE INDULT REGIME, 1985–2007

PROMPTED BY THE DEVELOPMENT OF THE traditionalist cause in Europe and especially in France, the Vatican had executed a remarkable about-face. It had extended permission to celebrate the old Roman Rite once again. Initially, by its very terms the permission was grudging. The local interpretations were even more restrictive. Later, *Ecclesia Dei* introduced a more generous policy.

Now although they had not done much to bring about this new situation, American Catholics were among the most active worldwide in taking advantage of it. They were aided by the prevailing spirit of the American hierarchy, which, although hostile, generally lacked the hard ideological edge found in France or Germany. The practical work of establishing traditional Mass apostolates also appealed to Americans. Whatever the cause, the effects were remarkable. By the end of the Indult period (2007) a very substantial portion of the American Catholic population had the traditional Mass available to it—at least if we define "available" to mean being subject to a drive of often two hours or more.

The locations and times of these indult Masses indeed often were selected to discourage attendance. Bishops would settle upon a church located in an unattractive or even dangerous part of town. Perhaps the ultimate expression of these policies was the indult Mass authorized in the Catholic chapel on the truly haunted grounds of the largely abandoned state insane asylum of Wingdale, New York. If the location was in a more normal parish setting, the very existence of the traditional liturgies often was concealed—indult Masses were usually not listed in parish bulletins. If the Mass could be celebrated on Sunday at all, the afternoon would almost inevitably be the only available slot—usually a great disadvantage for families with children.[1]

Attending these early Masses was often an adventure. Who, for example, can forget that first "authorized" traditional Mass in New York City, at old St. Ann's church on East 13th Street? Deliberately located in an out-of-the-way parish early Saturday afternoon (so the Sunday requirement could not be fulfilled), this first Mass nevertheless attracted a large crowd. Those who had shown up, however, found that the Archdiocese had prohibited the Mass at the last minute. But eventually that Mass did take place on a subsequent Saturday and, despite the adverse circumstances, the celebration of the traditional Mass continued in this church for many years afterwards.

The liturgical quality of these celebrations also often left something to be desired. The norm was the Low Mass. If possible, music would be tacked on, sometimes performed by a solo male cantor just like in preconciliar funerals. The celebrants' knowledge of the old rite, too, often left something to be desired.

So much could be expected. What was unexpected was the early appearance of a movement to restore the traditional liturgy to a completeness and magnificence far

---

[1] See Appendix I for examples of documents from the Indult period.

surpassing what had been the norm prior to the Council. Organizations and churches like the St. Gregory Society (New Haven) and St. John Cantius (Chicago) promoted the celebration of the liturgy with exactness of ritual (now and then even including the Solemn Mass) and with music performed on a professional level. How did this come about?

Perhaps the main reason was generational change. Traditionalists were of course disappointed that the indult found so little resonance among the general Catholic population. The twenty-year war of the establishment against Catholic Tradition had been successful to this extent: most Catholics had no interest in the traditional liturgy. Indeed, only a steadily declining minority of them had any interest in the Mass or the Church at all. But from the very beginning of the indult it was not just old-timers who were behind the return of the Latin Mass, but a younger generation, which could but dimly recall the preconciliar era—if they were old enough to have had any experience of those times at all. These young students, musicians, converts and priests had rediscovered the traditional faith often on their own—with God's help of course. If they were to celebrate the traditional Mass, they reasoned, it should be as perfect as possible. They rejected the shortcuts and compromises that had become all too prevalent in parish use prior to 1965. And, as with each year the number of these newcomers to Tradition grew, so did the perfection of the services as well. Thus, from the very beginning of the indult it was ludicrous to talk about "nostalgia" as the motivating factor of traditionalists (the party line of the clerical establishment and the Vatican).

Moreover, in the wake of *Ecclesia Dei* in 1988 the traditionalists received reinforcement in the form of a recognized clerical institute dedicated to Tradition yet in good standing with Rome—the Fraternity of St. Peter (FSSP).

It had broken away from the FSSPX over their ordination
of bishops. The arrival of the FSSP meant that the number
of churches where the liturgy would be celebrated in its
fullness would steadily increase. Regrettably, the FSSP,
riven by internal dissension and ideological conflicts,
proved unable to fulfill its potential role as unifier and
organizer of American traditionalist efforts. Perhaps we
see here also the continuation of an "American way" of
organization: the FSSPX likewise had failed to organize the
traditionalists just as Opus Dei (and all the other "ecclesial
movements") had failed to mobilize the "conservatives."

The work of restoring Tradition thus rested upon the
shoulders of a myriad of individual priests and laity, local
groups and societies. *Una Voce* in its latest incarnation
served as a helpful umbrella organization for some—but by
no means all—of these liturgical entrepreneurs and independent local chapters. Traditionalism in the United States
truly was a grass-roots effort dominated by the laity. Its
weakness was the divorce from the institutional Church and
the absence of any legal rights. Indult Masses remained a
mere gesture of tolerance subject to the arbitrary discretion
of each bishop or individual pastor. To cite one example,
a new indult Mass was established in 2005 in Saint Mary
of Stamford (near New York). A traditional community
developed and their liturgical life even culminated in the
celebration of a solemn pontifical Mass. In early 2007,
however, the pastor changed, and the new pastor summarily
terminated the indult Mass by the middle of that year. (Of
course, in many places this situation de facto continues to
the present day—compare similar experiences of the last
ten years at Our Saviour's in New York or at the Basilica
of Saint John the Evangelist in Stamford.)

Despite all the defects and limitations, the indult regime
had transformed the Catholic traditionalist movement.

Before the indult, American traditionalism, with the exception of the FSSPX, had been largely a theoretical discussion forum. After the indult it concentrated almost exclusively on the practical task of making the traditional liturgy available—with a great deal of success, all things considered. The achievement was attributable in large part to concentrating on the "single issue" of the liturgy—and ignoring most of the other myriad problems afflicting the Church.

For the "conservatives," the balance of these years was much more mixed in terms of practical consequences. And their most conspicuous failure was liturgical. In the name of authority, they (or the minority among them which was interested in such topics) had sallied forth against both the establishment and the progressives to challenge such things as communion in the hand and altar girls—only to have the Vatican pull the rug out from under their feet. In contrast to the conservatives' insistence on loyalty to a fixed liturgical text, the Vatican and the establishment repeatedly made it clear that the Novus Ordo would remain a "work in progress"—change would continue through a new praxis regardless of any texts or rules. At the other end of the liturgical spectrum, the coming of the indult—wholly unexpected by the conservatives—destroyed overnight interest in the Novus Ordo celebrated in Latin. In view of these developments the focus of the "liturgical conservatives" shifted from "strict construction" to "reform of the reform." That there were indeed problems in the current liturgy was now conceded; there was, however, no agreement on what the corrections should be.

In 1992 Roger McCaffrey launched a new magazine, *The Latin Mass*. In 1996 the same publisher launched a second magazine, *Sursum Corda. The Latin Mass*, aimed at traditionalists, concentrated on liturgy and aired broad issues of principle informed by a pessimistic, critical view

of Church and society. *Sursum Corda,* addressed to the
Catholic conservatives, emphasized the bright side, devoted
much space to concrete initiatives like homeschooling,
and featured accounts of the real or imaginary successes
of the contemporary Church. Two publications with the
same publisher and editor—what could illustrate better
the vast gap that had developed between the worldview
of traditionalism and that of conservative Catholicism?

Yet *The Latin Mass* had much greater significance. It
marked the first attempt since the demise of *Triumph*
to create a national forum on a high intellectual level
for traditionalism. After the years in "internal exile" and
the initial exclusive concentration on resurrecting the liturgy, traditionalists now sought both to consolidate their
achievements and return to the "public square" (using the
favorite metaphor of conservative Catholics).

The locations where traditional indult Masses were
celebrated continued to steadily increase. Traditional Catholics, however, were no longer satisfied merely with the
Mass. They wanted all the sacraments now. The drive for
all the sacraments actually dates to the first years of the
traditionalist revival under the indult. For example, in
1989 the Princeton University Chapel saw the celebration
of (supposedly) the first "officially authorized" traditional
Nuptial Mass in the United States since the 1960s. In a
very haphazard manner, celebration of the other sacraments
in the traditional rite also became generally available.

This all required increased dialogue with the institutional Church. Consequently, in many places a more
harmonious relationship with the local diocese developed.
Sitting bishops even celebrated the traditional Mass. As
time went on, indult traditional Catholicism became in
many areas of the United States a part of normal Catholic
life: limited in scale but real and accepted.

Further, the traditional Catholics wanted to establish fully functioning communities and parishes. In this period of consolidation that objective was achieved in a surprising number of locations. In this endeavor the recognized religious or clerical institutes—such as those recognized by the *Ecclesia Dei* commission—began to show their real value. It was one thing for the bishop to disregard the request of some group of laity—it was another matter to disregard the request of an order or community of priests recognized by Rome. In Chicago, for example, the clergy of the parish of St. John Cantius, site of an indult Mass, evolved in 1998 into an independent order, the Canons Regular of St. John Cantius. The Canons have as their mission "to help Catholics rediscover a profound sense of the sacred through solemn liturgies, devotions, sacred art and sacred music, as well as instruction in Church heritage, catechesis and Catholic culture in the context of parish ministry."[2] This alone shows the broadening horizons of the traditionalist movement. *Ecclesia Dei* communities such as the Priestly Fraternity of St. Peter, by 1995 joined by the Institute of Christ the King Sovereign Priest and then by others, although unable to provide overall direction to the traditionalist movement, were instrumental in establishing what were in reality traditionalist parishes, whatever their technical status in canon law. And in 1999, thirteen Benedictine monks from traditionalist Fontgombault Abbey established a Benedictine monastery in Clear Creek, Oklahoma. The new foundation, however, understood its heritage as also deriving from John Senior's Integrated Humanities Program.[3]

This turn outward was manifested in many activities. We have mentioned *The Latin Mass* magazine. Books of traditionalist authors also found an audience outside the

---

2 http://www.canons-regular.org/go/about/.
3 Bethel, *John Senior*, 1.

narrow circles of traditionalism itself. American traditionalists ventured out of their country in the early 1990s to
join the Chartres pilgrimage in France. Building on this,
they created their own "Pilgrimage for Restoration" to
the shrine of the North American martyrs in Auriesville,
New York. At the conclusion of the first pilgrimage, several
thousand participants witnessed the first Solemn High
Mass at the shrine since the Second Vatican Council.

And there were even more spectacular examples of
success. On May 12, 1996, a traditional Mass was held for
the first time in many decades in St. Patrick's Cathedral
in New York City—celebrated by Cardinal Alfons Maria
Stickler before a standing-room-only congregation of over
four thousand. In 2004, *The Passion of the Christ*, directed
by Mel Gibson of the "Trotskyite" (sedevacantist) wing of
traditionalism, achieved the greatest national and international success of any religious film in decades.

Regrettably, towards the end of the indult era the
relationship of traditionalists with conservative Catholics
steadily worsened despite (or because of?) the growing
institutional and societal recognition of the traditionalist
movement. After innumerable reverses and disappoint-
ments—we need cite only the hierarchy's contemptuous
treatment of the founders of both EWTN and Ignatius
Press—a significant faction among the conservatives paradoxically adopted a much more conciliatory tone with the
establishment. The intensifying sexual abuse crisis would
seem to have confirmed the dire predictions of conservative
Catholics over the years, and some conservatives indeed
understood it as such. Others, however, now rallied to
the episcopal establishment, minimizing the extent of the
crisis or damning the news media.

Conservative Catholic works (like George Weigel's biog-
raphy of John Paul II) began to be mentioned with favor

in the Vatican—at least to the extent they seemed to support the institution. The Legionaries of Christ were now attempting to organize conservative Catholics, particularly in the homeschooling movement, through Regnum Christi. And this developing rapprochement with the establishment and its policies also led to some interesting interactions with the conservatives' mortal enemy, the progressives (consider the 2005 book on Opus Dei commissioned by them, authored by John Allen of the *National Catholic Reporter*).

It was in this context that the internet appeared on the scene. It would have revolutionary consequences for the ability of Catholics to communicate with each other outside of the progressive news media or the official Catholic press. As could be expected, conservative Catholics were initially more active in utilizing the new medium. Partly as a consequence of the arrival of the internet and the unrestrained discourse of some of the conservative "players," however, the dislike of leading conservatives for traditional Catholics grew to something that could only be called hatred.

There were other concerns for traditionalists in what otherwise could be taken as an era of maturity and consolidation. Traditionalists remained very much a tolerated minority in most dioceses, under close supervision. In certain places—including the chapels of some prominent conservative Catholic colleges—the traditional Mass continued to be banned altogether; in other dioceses the *Ecclesia Dei* institutes remained excluded. The New York clerical establishment saw to it that the 1996 Mass at St. Patrick's Cathedral was never repeated. *The Latin Mass* magazine eventually merged with *Sursum Corda*. After coming under new management, it remained a solid publication but no longer aspired to provide any overall leadership.

The growing "normality" of traditionalism regrettably also meant that some of the worst ills of the contemporary

Church made their appearance in the traditionalist world as well. If we consider the "Society of St. John" to be traditionalist (established in 1998, they used a "1965" missal instead of the "preconciliar" 1962 missal) we see how the sexual abuse scandals could intrude into traditionalism and have the same devastating impact as they did in the "conciliar Church" as a whole. In this case not only did the Society of St. John itself collapse but the scandalous deeds of some of its leaders did irreparable harm to a neighboring traditionalist secondary school as well.

In view of these developments, is it surprising that, towards the end of this era, certain traditionalists started to waver? Several noted traditionalist spokesmen moved over to sedevacantism—a temptation perhaps stronger in the United States than elsewhere in the world. In a sense, sedevacantism was a return to the pre-indult "ghetto" to preserve an imaginary purity. Paradoxically it also reveals, though, the underlying traditionalist dissatisfaction with the entire indult regime of mere liturgical "tolerance," however great the accomplishments under it had been. *The Latin Mass* magazine had described itself as a "chronicle of a Catholic reform." Perhaps most American traditionalists were still unable to articulate their principles and aims that clearly. But traditionalism was on the point of awakening to serve as a potential influence for change for the entire Church.

4 *Liberation!*

SUMMORUM PONTIFICUM, 2007–2013

O N JULY 7, 2007, POPE BENEDICT XVI issued *motu proprio* his apostolic letter *Summorum Pontificum*. For traditionalists it was a vindication and emancipation that would have been scarcely imaginable a few short years before. Now, the traditional liturgy was acknowledged to be a constituent element of the Catholic faith that had not been and could not be abrogated. The traditional liturgy was declared a right of the faithful. They, not the hierarchy and the clergy, were empowered to request and obtain its celebration. Finally, an avenue of appeal to Rome was provided in the (all too likely) case of conflicts with the local hierarchy.

Less obviously revolutionary but perhaps even more significant in the long term was Pope Benedict's December 22, 2005 discourse on the "hermeneutic of reform in continuity." By emphasizing the need to understand "the Council" (there seems to be only one in the Church of today) in the light of the entirety of the Tradition and doctrine of the Church, Pope Benedict was (undoubtedly unwittingly) calling the whole Conciliar project into question. For isn't the real essence of "Vatican II" the opening of a supposedly moribund and retrograde Church to the

33

new truths and vitality proceeding from an unprecedented and revolutionary modernity?

What was the impact of these momentous developments in the United States? Compared to the spirit and even the letter of the new law it was, of course, limited. If traditionalists expected the hierarchy suddenly to take the initiative to make the traditional liturgy broadly available, they would be sorely disappointed. In most cases, after *Summorum Pontificum* the bishop no longer "got in the way" of local traditionalist initiatives.

In the New York area, for example, it was only a few parishes that immediately and completely "implemented" *Summorum Pontificum*. In most cases episcopal monitoring and authorization continued. As one wag put it, under *Summorum Pontificum* the hierarchy finally discovered the Indult. So, Charles Chaput, the newly installed archbishop of Philadelphia, made a parish available to traditionalists— while describing the motu proprio in language precisely fitting the former Indult.

Yet even this minimum was of course a dramatic transformation. The traditional Mass now reappeared all over the Catholic landscape, resurfacing in locations previously unimaginable: Jesuit universities, cathedrals, campus chapels, churches of religious orders and even the parishes of the well-to-do. The mainstream Catholic press now actually began to report traditional liturgies and events and did so in a neutral, even respectful tone. Even the institutions of "conservative Catholicism" which only yesterday had been conducting a bitter war of words with traditionalists now opened their doors—at least partially—to the old Mass: e.g., Thomas Aquinas College, Ave Maria University.

But the change in the quality of the liturgies was even more significant than the growth of their number. The traditionalists of 2007 did not aim at recreating some past they had never known; they wanted to restore the rites of the Catholic Church in all their splendor. The Solemn High Mass—which prior to the Council and in the Indult era was a rarity—now was celebrated often, in a few places even every Sunday. Solemn Pontifical Masses became, at least in the greater New York area, almost an annual event. Vespers, which had disappeared from the American scene—at least on the parish level—well before the Council, here and there now sprang back to life. There was, in all these liturgical efforts, a new insistence on perfection and completeness of the ceremonial, the music, the vestments and the very furnishing and arrangements of the churches.

There was a significant shift in leadership as well. Spear-heading the era of *Summorum Pontificum* was a generation of young priests—in contrast with the overwhelmingly lay leadership of all previous phases of the American tradition-alist movement and despite the emphasis of *Summorum Pontificum* on the initiative of lay communities. These priests, born years after the Vatican Council, had no knowledge of preconciliar times. In many cases they lacked extensive experience of even the Indult era. They were joined by older priests "young at heart"—ordained well after the Council but unacquainted with anything prior to it. Together, it was a generation that had observed for itself what was going on (mostly wrongly) with the Church and had rediscovered Tradition through the example of others, through reading or through—let us acknowledge it—the workings of Divine Providence. They now joyfully responded to Pope Benedict's invitation. An ever-growing number of seminarians also became interested in the traditional Mass. Finally, even the mainstream religious orders—a territory which, except for isolated individuals, had remained off limits to conservatism, let alone traditionalism—now participated at least to some extent in the traditionalist revival. Certain of these orders (like the Dominicans) even had their own rites which were now celebrated regularly for the first time in decades.

Not that the "traditionalist tradition" of lay leadership had entirely come to an end. On the contrary: *Summorum Pontificum* saw a new generation of Catholic lay organizations arise. Moreover, the stability of these groupings was far greater than that of their "conservative Catholic" counterparts (and traditionalist predecessors) because of their devotion to the objective liturgical tradition of the Church and their new links with the existing structures of the Church.

The result was a much greater integration of the traditionalist movement into the day-to-day life of the "American Catholic Church." There was a new willingness to compromise and to work out a *modus vivendi* of the various liturgical directions within the Church. More and more parishes became de facto "biritual" without awakening the divisive ideological debates of the past. Despite much nonsense written at the beginning, it soon became clear that the old and new rites, the old and new calendars could very well coexist. Recourse to the appeal mechanisms provided by *Summorum Pontificum* was—in number of respects, fortunately—not a normal feature of post-motu proprio life in the United States.

The "fruits of *Summorum Pontificum*" were not long in coming. For example, Saint Mary's parish in Norwalk, Connecticut offered both the ordinary and the extraordinary forms. But it was the traditional Mass around which the life of the parish soon oriented. There followed greater involvement of the laity in the life of this parish, its music, its devotions and its liturgies; more frequent reception of the sacrament of confession; and that ultimate criterion of Catholic success, increased amounts in the collection basket. The interior of St. Mary's, which had been gutted and then timidly refurbished in the postconciliar decades, was now lavishly redecorated. Vocations of course also appeared. The traditional liturgy, far from being a source of division, became a source of unification of a parish otherwise divided into number of isolated communities: Hispanics, Indians, old-time Italian and Irish parishioners, etc.

A unique and moving measure of this parish's success was two dramatic deathbed testimonies in favor of the traditional liturgy—including the request for a Requiem Mass—by two prominent parishioners who had had no connection with traditionalism until the era of *Summorum Pontificum*. Perhaps the greatest testimony to the success of St. Mary's under the motu proprio is that of all those most directly involved with the work of the parish—the clergy, the ministers, the musicians, the lay volunteers—only two or three had any experience with the preconciliar Church or even any long-term experience of the Indult.

Returning to the national scene, a further benefit of the new regime of *Summorum Pontificum* was the cooling off of the cold war waged by conservative Catholics against the traditionalist movement. Indeed, some prominent publicists of "conservative Catholicism" and "Reform of the Reform" increasingly became supporters of the new course. Others, who could not disguise their disagreement with Benedict's motu proprio, retreated into silence: in keeping with their principles how could they dispute any action taken by the pope?

It will be noted that the era of *Summorum Pontificum* was once more primarily liturgical: the invitation of Pope Benedict to reflect upon the relationship of the Council to the whole course of Catholic Tradition was not immediately taken up in the United States. Since the fall of *Triumph* there was no publication or organization exercising intellectual leadership on these shores. The intellectual component of traditionalism was still overwhelmingly provided by foreign sources—German, French, English, and increasingly Italian.

But one positive development in all this was the blossoming of the traditionalist internet scene. Through sites and blogs traditionalists obtained unprecedented access to news of the Church and the intellectual developments abroad. Moreover, in the post-*Summorum Pontificum* "era of good feeling" certain key players of the "conservative Catholic" internet now joined in publicizing traditionalist developments.

Yet all was not sweetness and light. There were disturbing shadows of the past, and, in hindsight, somber forebodings of the future. The implementation of *Summorum Pontificum* was very uneven—the attitude towards the traditional liturgy in many dioceses remained resolutely hostile. Seminarians and members of religious orders regularly faced sanctions for participating in traditional liturgies. It still remained common for clergy and aspiring clerics to request anonymity if they showed up in the sanctuary for a traditionalist service.

In 2010, for example, a magnificent pontifical liturgy was scheduled at the Shrine of the Immaculate Conception in Washington, DC. The Archbishop of Washington prevented the participation by the scheduled celebrant, Cardinal Darío Castrillón Hoyos.[1] The next year, Archbishop Wuerl forced the cancellation at the last minute of the scheduled Pontifical Mass. It has not reappeared since.[2]

Moreover, towards the end of this period, the underground forces opposed to *Summorum Pontificum* seem to have regrouped both in the United States and in the Vatican. For example, the worldwide crisis in the Franciscan Friars of the Immaculate—an order which had elected to be biritual—was launched with the key participation of certain American members and the encouragement of

---

[1] It was celebrated instead by the Most Rev. Edward Slattery.

[2] Several years after this article was written, on April 28, 2018, Archbishop Alexander K. Sample celebrated a solemn Pontifical Mass at the high altar of the Shrine, and on November 16, 2019, Archbishop Salvatore Cordileone did the same.

certain "conservative Catholic" veterans.

That there were also issues within the traditionalist movement itself cannot be denied. A certain lassitude seems to have overtaken many of the traditionalists. Instead of redoubling their efforts and eagerly seizing the incredible opportunities now made available to them to both celebrate the traditional liturgy and evangelize others, many were willing to sit back and let the clergy take over the running of the traditionalist show. This passive, inwardly focused attitude, so typical of mainstream American Catholicism, could only be disastrous for a still marginalized movement like traditionalism. For as subsequent events would show, official favor can be a very fleeting thing. It is a sad fact that many promising traditionalist liturgical initiatives had to be abandoned because of lack of participation.

Do we also need to mention that some of the negative organizational features of the Indult era continued? That no publication of a high level existed that would serve to focus traditional Catholics and inform them of developments? That traditionalists continued to be divided into many different groupings under dominating leaders—either lay or clerical? That it was nearly impossible to get these groups to even inform each other of what they were doing, let alone collaborate and cooperate? These long-standing difficulties remained—yet it was reasonable to hope that they would be worked out in the course of time.

In summary, traditionalists had indeed accomplished something tremendous. A cause that had been written off as dead and been subjected to the almost universal opposition of the Church establishment had been resurrected. And, most importantly, fifty years after the close of the Vatican Council, the traditionalist movement had been handed over to a new generation—one untainted by the complexes and compromises of the past.

5 *Progressivism Prevails*

THE FIRST FOUR YEARS OF FRANCIS'S PAPACY, 2013–2017

ONCE AGAIN THE TRADITIONALIST scene in the United States was rocked by an event from across the seas. Pope Benedict, who had done so much for the cause of Catholic Tradition—without ever fully embracing it himself—abdicated. It was clear from the start that his successor, Francis, would be a man of entirely different character. Had he not been promoted as the main alternative to Benedict in the 2005 conclave? But what few knew—aside from a key group of initiates—was that Francis was a genuine progressive along the lines of Cardinals Bernardin and Martini. What had been inconceivable in 1978 or 2005 had taken place: the far left wing of the Church had captured its highest position.

If we consider things only from the American perspective, this development, while unexpected, was not at all surprising. For the Church's progressive wing in the United States had not been idle in the years over which we have followed the twists and turns of traditionalism. They remained in total control of most religious orders and Catholic institutions of higher education. The Catholic press and the Church bureaucracy were in their hand. And they retained vocal supporters among the hierarchy like Mahoney, Bernardin, and Weakland while representatives of the clerical "power elite" like McCarrick and Wuerl provided assistance.

Beyond maintaining their position within the Church, the Catholic left forged powerful links with the forces of civil society. They developed valuable ties with the secular educational establishment. The liberal media (that is, almost all the media) turned to the progressive agitators for "authoritative" commentary on things Catholic; even the Catholic hierarchy (including the Vatican) turned to the *National Catholic Reporter* as the preferred media outlet. And a new field of activity for the progressives was the overt alliance with the Democratic Party and specifically the Obama administration, counteracting "pro-life" initiatives in and outside of the Church. Popes John Paul II and Benedict attempted to restrain American Catholic progressivism, but both lacked the will to discipline, let alone dislodge it.

Pope Francis immediately launched a systematic campaign both of accommodation with Western secular civil society and of outreach to the Catholic left. Certainly, in rhetoric it has been a return to the 1960s, as covered in the first chapter of this essay. Instead of increasingly respectful treatment, traditionalists now heard themselves denounced by Pope Francis in coarse and contemptuous language. More concretely, at Francis's direction, the Vatican launched a campaign of annihilation against the Franciscan Friars of the Immaculate—a biritual order with a growing traditionalist commitment. One of the main initial penalties imposed was the *de facto* abolition of *Summorum Pontificum* for these friars. It was soon succeeded by attacks on other traditionalist institutions. But these actions initially had little resonance in the United States, given the limited presence here of these communities.

The forces of the American "conservative Catholics" had very little time to rejoice, however, at the discomfiture of the traditionalists. For Francis and his acolytes immediately moved, in word and deed, even more radically against the holiest principles of the conservatives. Francis and his team denounced capitalist economic principles. They called into question or mocked pro-life activity of all kinds. Memorably, they termed the cooperation between Protestant fundamentalists and conservative Catholics an "alliance of hate." Both Francis and his entourage spoke with barely concealed animosity of Americans. And as one of his first initiatives, Pope Francis launched a "discussion" clearly aiming at changing the rules of the Church regarding divorce. This last move struck the weakest link in the conservatives' stance on life issues. For divorce is an unambiguous conflict between the teaching of the Church and one of the nonnegotiable principles of American civil society.

What was the impact of these dramatic developments? We have seen that in the 1960s the reforms of the Council had been virtually unopposed. The reaction to the current attempted restoration of the 1960s has been far more complex. True, among the (active) clergy open rebellion is nonexistent. Yet by 2013 a lively Catholic samizdat—by way of the Internet—had arisen. News was rapidly disseminated, and critical commentary offered. The traditionalist Catholic of 2013 had an infinitely better idea of what was going on in the Church—both in and outside of the United States—than his predecessor of fifty years ago. And his experience of fifty years of working around the structures of the "official Church" had immunized him against the progressive revival.

There is above all this remarkable fact: under Francis the traditionalist cause in America has actually *strengthened*. True, certain Masses sponsored by "fair-weather friends" were canceled. But other Masses and apostolates have taken their place. Certain prelates took the opportunity to settle scores with a movement they always disdained. But others have maintained and even expanded the traditionalist presence in their dioceses. Traditional Masses are still spreading to new locations with full official support. The successful *modus vivendi* of traditional Catholicism with the Church establishment, inaugurated by *Summorum Pontificum*, has largely continued. For traditionalists, the loss of papal support has not produced an existential crisis or a rush to "preemptive obedience" (as the Germans call it).

The situation of the conservative Catholics is much more dire. For Pope Francis has radically challenged their core beliefs on the nature of the papacy, the role of the United States, "life issues," and the economy. Only a minority (of which George Weigel is representative) attempted at first to uphold the ultramontane cause in its purity, seeking to prove that Francis was no different than Benedict, John Paul II, or Paul VI. Other leading spokesmen lapsed into silence or vehemently criticized the utterances of the pope's inner circle (but, initially, not those of Francis himself). We do observe, however, that the pro-life movement continued in its accustomed course, unconcerned about whether they are "obsessing" (Pope Francis's term) or not.

But, of course, the main threat hanging over the traditionalists' heads is the threat of Pope Francis. The Pope regularly denounces traditionalists, in uncouth but unambiguous language, as mentally ill and worse. And the sycophants of Francis, both in and outside of the Vatican, have amplified his words. It has not eluded them—nor their master—that so many of the opponents of Francis's regime have connections to the world of traditionalism. We also have to consider the long-term effect of the endless

stream of hostile statements from the Vatican and of potential episcopal appointments as well.

Outside the United States, the Vatican has struck again
and again with utter ruthlessness at smaller traditionalist
seminaries, orders, and congregations. The pope recently
has abolished the *Ecclesia Dei* commission (charged with
certain supervisory and appeals functions under *Summorum
Pontificum* that were rarely exercised), but we do not yet
know the exact intent of that step. In the United States
itself, we have the actions of Cardinal Cupich, Bergoglio's
main paladin in the American hierarchy, against the leadership of the parish of St. John Cantius.

Any more general action the Pope might take restricting
the old liturgy would be unlikely to encounter any organized episcopal opposition. For if Bergoglio has demon-
strated conclusively one thing over the last six years, it is
that, aside from individual exceptions, the hierarchs of
the Catholic Church will not oppose anything he says or
does. Yet, so far, the Pope has not sought to impose any
restrictions on the celebration of the traditional liturgy.[1]

Recently certain prominent traditionalists seem to have
lost their heads over this situation, predicting the imminent
demise of the traditional Mass or of *Summorum Pontificum*
due to a papal prohibition. I am not so sure! Are not these
voices still imprisoned in the Ultramontane world, where
everything depends on official support and papal favor?
We have seen how American traditionalism has survived
and even flourished in the last six years. And, paradoxically, hasn't the papacy of Francis had a liberating effect
on traditionalism? A Pope, for example, who from the
earliest days of his pontificate so prominently disregards
liturgical norms, also empowers traditionalists to "do the

[1] As of 2017, when this column was published. *Traditionis Custodes*
is taken up in the last chapter.

right thing" liturgically instead of anxiously pondering issues of rubrics, authority, and legality.

We do not know what the future will bring. We do not know what will happen if Francis extends in some way the actions he has taken against the Franciscan Friars of the Immaculate to the whole Church. My personal view is that Francis's actions on other fronts (such as on divorce, homosexuality, and clerical celibacy) will precipitate such a crisis in the Church that the relationship with traditionalists will remain in the background. Moreover, Vatican financial scandals and the Pope's mishandling of clerical sexual abuse have shaken even the strongest pillars holding up Bergoglianism—the Western secular media. It would be just as plausible, however, that if the Pope suffers a reverse on these other issues, he would respond by retaliating against "enemies"—of which traditionalists would be the easiest and safest targets. I do believe, however, that, whatever may come, a movement that by now is so broad in its membership and support will continue, in whatever ways open to it, the slow but relentless course of renewal and reform.

6 *The Era of Pope Francis*

FOUR YEARS LATER, 2017–2020

L AST YEAR, BEFORE DAWN IN THE SEASON of Advent, the following scene was enacted in many parishes. In the darkness of the church the only illumination is the glow of massed candles surrounding the altar—the priest and ministers performing the ceremonies are silhouetted against this mysterious light. A music more somber than usual is heard and in the obscurity the fragrance of the incense seems stronger. Only as the pale light of dawn spreads do the windows, statues, and paintings emerge. It is the celebration of a *Rorate* Mass during Advent. An old custom, revived in a handful of churches after the promulgation of *Summorum Pontificum,* has now spread everywhere in the traditionalist world—and, judging from recent photographs, well beyond that. The bulk of this growth has been just in the last four or five years.

The rediscovery of this ancient custom perfectly illustrates the maturity of the traditionalist movement. Other examples abound: the revival of sung Vespers at the parish level, the use of the folded chasuble, and, most notably, the celebration of the "pre-1955" Holy Week rites. I don't think it is an exaggeration to state that today's liturgical celebrations are in every way more complete and precise than was the case in all but a handful of places before the Council. Moreover, the atmosphere of legalism, fault-finding, capriciousness, and eccentricity that used to characterize discussions within traditionalism have yielded to a focus on understanding the meaning of the ceremonies and, to the extent resources permit, achieving their completeness and perfection. It is a true renaissance—the "recovery of the sacred"!

The progress of the movement has continued unabated. We see it in the increasing number and quality of the celebrations of the traditional Mass this year. We see it in the ongoing interest of so many seminarians in the Old Rite despite the obstacles often put in their path. We see it in the parishes—usually those that have chosen to celebrate the traditional Mass frequently and regularly—that gather large regular congregations for the Latin Mass.

A glance at those pews reveals that most of the faithful have come back to Tradition in the last 20 or so years—and many more recently than that. For by now the handover of the cause of Tradition to a new generation is all but complete; in the sanctuary newly ordained priests and youthful ministers are assuming leadership roles. Indeed, we now encounter here and there young Catholics who have been raised in traditional Catholicism over the last fifteen to twenty years! This is not to disparage in any way those (like me) who had experienced the traditional Mass prior to the revolution of the Council and who have "fought the good fight" over the long years prior to *Summorum Pontificum* or even *Ecclesia Dei*. But we must acknowledge that by now a new generation has achieved a higher level of understanding and practice.

As has always been the case, American traditionalists do not stand alone. As a rule, they follow with great interest developments outside their parish, diocese, and even country. Scholars, writers, religious, and bishops from

other countries regularly visit these shores. The network
of websites and blogs which serve as Catholic samizdat
continues to perform invaluable service in this regard. It is
all a strong contrast with the provincialism of the average
layman in a Novus Ordo parish.

A continuing benefit of the current pontificate is the
almost complete disintegration of "conservative Catholicism" as writer after writer has been compelled to take
a stand against the policies of Pope Francis. Not that
these figures have become traditionalists! But at least the
decades-long cold war between traditionalists and "conservatives" is now largely a thing of the past. George Weigel
may continue to take swipes against "the traditionalist
millennial who has no idea why Vatican II was necessary"—what a bizarre statement indeed!—but he is now
in the minority. And even Weigel himself has reached the
limit of his tolerance for the present Vatican—although
he still will not criticize the Pope!

The Priestly Fraternity of St. Pius X (FSSPX) and the
Ecclesia Dei communities have continued to make steady
advances: increasing numbers of priests and seminarians,
new seminaries and new pastoral undertakings. We even
hear that not all those wishing to become seminarians
can be accommodated! It must be said, however, that
it is primarily the Institute of Christ the King Sovereign
Priest, which has grasped fully the new possibilities open
to traditionalism after *Summorum Pontificum*. Displaying
a welcome flair for publicity—restoring magnificent old
churches and celebrating splendid liturgies—they have not
been afraid to reach out to the broader traditionalist and
even non-Christian world. In contrast, the Fraternity of
St. Peter seems still locked in the closed, non-evangelical
pre-*Summorum Pontificum* world of the Indult. And even
the FSSPX—apparently mesmerized by the never-ending

discussions with Rome pursuing the will o' the wisp of their full regularization—is keeping a much lower profile than did their founder in the 1970s and 80s.

But additional spiritual resources also have emerged. The Benedictine monastery of Norcia, located in Italy but with mostly American monks, has exercised a worldwide influence. And that not just within Catholic traditionalism—do we need to mention its prominence in a certain widely publicized book discussing current options for Christians?[1] In the United States itself, a series of female convents and monasteries are now exclusively traditionalist. The expansion of traditionalist contemplative life is a lesser known but monumental step forward.

So, a movement that first arose out of the religious chaos of the postconciliar years finds itself an established, if marginal, part of the United States Catholic scene. In a way, Pope Francis should be happy with the traditionalists; their only method of survival and of evangelization has been by means of example. Without the institutional support of the hierarchy, the Catholic educational system, or the religious orders, the traditionalists built a network for themselves. It is growing, not receding. In many, if not most places, a working relationship has been established with the institutional Church. And leadership has been handed over to a new generation of clergy, religious, and laity. It is a success envied by traditionalists in other parts of the world.

Not all is rosy in the traditionalist world—far from it. If anyone thought traditionalism would free Catholics from the administrative incompetence, materialism, personality conflicts, jealousies, rivalries, and general human failings, both great and small, that have dogged the Church since

---

1 I am referring to *The Benedict Option* by Rod Dreher (New York: Penguin Random House, 2017). The author does not mention that Norcia is traditionalist.

its inception—he soon found out otherwise. More specifically to traditionalism, the celebration of the old Mass
remains under restriction and close supervision in many
dioceses in the United States. Seminarians often face
hurdles in participating in Latin Masses; some members
of mainstream orders who celebrate the traditional Mass
don't want to be photographed or identified. Ecclesiastical
favor or disfavor is all very random and often changes
month to month. And *Summorum Pontificum* traditionalists
are particularly exposed to the whims of pastors. In New
Jersey a dispute about the length of the traditional Mass
celebrations resulted in the ejection of a flourishing traditionalist community from its home parish. In Connecticut,
one of the leading traditionalist parishes has been racked
by controversy after a change in pastor. Traditionalists are
aware that they remain the one group within the Roman
Catholic Church that can be officially persecuted. It is
frustrating that, after so many years and so much effort,
traditionalists remain very much on the outside.

Part of the discontent is the pain of honestly facing the
reality of the "Conciliar Church"; the dire past predictions
of the traditionalists have only been proved so terribly true.
This is a Church where the knowledge of religion among
the mass of Catholics borders on the nonexistent; where
the practice of the overwhelming majority in key areas of
morality is hardly distinct from that of the surrounding
population. A Church whose hierarchy seems "obsessed"
only with material, secular issues and with arranging their
comfortable accommodation with the world. A Church
where the pope, the Vatican, and the bulk of the hierarchy are able to isolate themselves in a fantasy world, free
both from the obligation of dealing with reality and from
accountability for their actions. A Church that expressly
rejects the rational and the beautiful, patronizing instead

anti-intellectual "movements." A Church that at the highest level now openly propagates an anti-Christian morality and theology. A Church that is on the path to extinction in the developed world (and in Latin America as well).

The unavoidable issue is that, faced with such challenges and given its principles, traditionalism cannot remain the province of a nostalgic few, of a "remnant" or of an elite following a "counsel of perfection." Traditionalism can be nothing else than how it was described in the subtitle of *Latin Mass* magazine: a "movement for Catholic reform." Not a call back to some past which never existed but a rediscovery and reliving, in all its neglected richness and completeness, of the Tradition of the Church. To live completely the liturgical life of the church necessarily is inseparable from adhering to Christian morality and accepting Christian theology.

There is more than enough to do in rebuilding the Church, but isn't it clear that Catholic traditionalism also has important consequences for the life of the Catholic in the world and in this country? Certainly, our secular adversaries think so—that is why Pope Benedict faced opposition not just from within the Church but from secular governments and from Western civil society in general. It is very important to the governing secular forces in the Western world that the progress of the traditionalist cause be stopped—the Latin Mass is a political issue!

What is the next step for the traditionalists confronted by both the great promise of their movement and the catastrophic situation of the Church today? There have been many heroic laymen and priests in the American traditionalist movement; there have been many intrepid writers, journalists and, today, bloggers. And there has been an ever-increasing focus on the liturgy in all its perfection. But I believe to get to the next step, to become a genuine reform for the whole Church, the traditionalist movement needs to acquire what ancient Ireland is reputed to have had when it set out to re-evangelize the West: saints and scholars. Let us take that in reverse order.

Scholars are easiest to develop and train. They need to acquire the tools of scholarship in their various fields without becoming a part of a toxic secular academic establishment. Scholars can preserve and present to clergy and laity the riches of Catholic history, philosophy, and theology. They can deal squarely with the unpleasant truths of the past and the present, which Catholics make a habit of ignoring. They will counter the normal Catholic response when confronted by difficulties of all kinds: the flight to the irrational, blind submission to the world or to ecclesiastical authorities.

Saints—that is another matter. The crisis of the Church in the sixteenth century was overcome through a new generation of saints. When, in the 1520s, things were at their bleakest, a soldier, Ignatius Loyola, was reading a book of saints while recovering from a war wound. A little while later John Fisher and Thomas More stood virtually alone against the conformism of the hierarchy of an entire kingdom. Later there were many more: like the mystics Teresa of Avila and John of the Cross, the great Archbishop of Milan Charles Borromeo, and the apostle of Rome Saint Philip Neri. But saints cannot be "produced"—they can only be given to us.

Is my vision—scholarship and sanctity added to liturgical perfection—not unlike the Benedictine reform of the sixth century onwards? Does not American traditionalism need more focus on contemplation as opposed to action? I do believe so! But I would also expect that the traditionalist movement, which has overcome so many difficulties and challenges to reach where it stands today, will enjoy the necessary divine support to continue and perfect its mission—if we only ask and pray for it.

7 Catholic Traditionalism in the Coronavirus World

2020-2021

IN THE FIRST HALF OF 2020, LIFE IN THE developed world came to a shuddering standstill. The pleasant cocoon surrounding the populations of Western Europe and the United States seemed to disintegrate and apocalyptic hysteria seized the upper hand. The media and forces of the establishment, for their own reasons and based on murky data, seized the opportunity to whip collective fears into a fever heat. Suddenly a culture devoted exclusively to money, sex, pleasure, and bodily health had hit a road mine. The denizens of the global society without limits had to confront limitations—even, at least in their own minds, the possibility of imminent death. Overnight a quasi-totalitarian regime was imposed, in which the state was empowered to regulate, in the greatest possible detail, public, business, religious, and even personal life. (Here in Connecticut, for example, the governor devoted considerable efforts to deciding whether beauty salons can use blow dryers.) We are slowly re-emerging "from under the rubble" of the pandemic. Yet within days a new crisis has been ignited.

As we have done almost every year since 2013, we will reflect upon the current status of the Catholic traditionalist movement; its successes, failures, and outlook. What are

53

the next steps for traditionalists seven years into the pontificate of Francis? Although we confine our efforts to the
United States, of necessity these reflections will stray, as
appropriate, from the narrow confines of the "American
Catholic Church."

Regarding the Church, we can only record the abysmal
failure of the hierarchy, of the Catholic institutions, and
of the Pope. In the greatest domestic crisis in decades,
the clergy have been silent, the state discontinuing their
"services" as "non-essential"—with their own concurrence.
Nor did we see a wave of discontent about that among the
laity, as, depending on the location, churches were locked,
Masses were suspended, and some or all of the sacraments
were withheld. Catholics died in hospitals and nursing
homes alone without the presence of their family or clergy
and bereft of prayers or the sacraments. The hierarchy took
its direction from the media, the government bureaucrats,
the scientists and, to the extent avoidance of liability was
involved, the lawyers. Right now the dioceses of the New
York area are issuing page after page of regulations on
the resumption of Masses and the sacraments, which are
obviously more concerned with avoiding legal exposure
than the good of souls.

The permanent damage of these days will be enormous.
For in all honesty, is not sheer inertia the greatest force
propping up the post-Vatican II Church among the laity?
How many of the minority which still regularly attends
Mass will return after this interruption of months? And
how many others will remember with resentment the pas-
sivity of their shepherds? At a minimum, an institutional
decline that has assumed record levels under Pope Francis
will only accelerate.

But where does Catholic traditionalism itself stand?
Before the grand shutdown, celebrations of the traditional

Mass had been growing by leaps and bounds both in quantity and quality. The movement had been successfully passed on to a new generation of priests and laity. Monasteries such as Silverstream or Norcia—situated outside the US but closely linked to US traditionalism—were flourishing, overcoming incredible obstacles of all kinds. At home, the celebration of the traditional Mass had moved into cathedrals and basilicas. It seemed that each year brought new accomplishments. In the New York area, early 2020 saw not just one but two solemn pontifical Masses celebrated by cardinals. Just recently even *The New York Times* had to acknowledge—viewed from their perspective of course—the new popularity of Catholic Tradition among younger "weird" Catholics.[1] Meanwhile, traditionalists assumed more and more the role of leaders of the overall Catholic right as their conservative allies (and erstwhile adversaries) fell into ever greater confusion and intellectual chaos in the face of the unshakably radical course of Pope Francis & Co. Indeed, a sign of the maturity of the traditionalist movement today is its independence from the need of Vatican favor. If fifteen or twenty years ago traditionalist events such as the annual Chartres pilgrimage felt compelled to insinuate—falsely—in words and images that Pope John Paul II supported their endeavors, I doubt anyone would make the same claim today for Francis!

Yet the great coronavirus panic largely brought the celebration of the traditional Mass to a halt. We have seen the vitality of the movement, however, in the high number of traditional Masses that have been streamed in these dark days. And traditional priests—at least some of them—have been more willing than the others to bend the rules to keep at least some semblance of the sacraments available.

---

1   Tara Isabella Burton, "Christianity Gets Weird," *The New York Times*, May 8, 2020.

Let's also not forget that—even if it happened outside
the United States—it was the French traditionalists, not
the indifferent French hierarchy, which obtained in court
the reversal of state measures restricting the celebration
of the Mass in that country. Nevertheless, traditionalists
too will face fallout arising from their conduct during
the pandemic.

More regrettably, the last year has seen an outbreak
of bitter infighting among traditionalists themselves on a
national, regional, and local level. Once more the FSSPX
has become a target. Conflicts have erupted routinely
on occasions great and small. Some of this is a natural
consequence of growth, as traditionalists deepen their
interaction with each other, the rest of the Church, and
the world and encounter new and unanticipated points of
friction. But much of the current agitation arises from sheer
stupidity and inability to subordinate individual wishes and
grievances to the common good of Catholic traditionalism.

The institutional adversaries of the Old Mass have
hardly been inactive either. As the traditional Mass gains
greater visibility in the "Catholic public square," the mach-
inations and maneuvers of the Catholic establishment
against traditionalism continue and even intensify. In
some cases, perhaps unsurprisingly, the instigators of anti-
traditionalist vendettas were not the clergy but the aging
laity of the Vatican II generation. Here a traditionalist
professor is forced out of a "Catholic" college; there a
traditionalist priest is dismissed from his parish and made
chaplain of a nursing home. Diocesan clergy committed
to celebrating the traditional Mass are subject to all kinds
of harassment and chicanery, while certain priests who
only occasionally celebrate the traditional Mass continue
to demand that they not be identified or photographed.
There have been instances where the traditional Mass,

even a Nuptial Mass, could only be celebrated on a semi-clandestine basis.[2]

We have previously spoken of the hostility of the current pontiff to the traditional Mass—I don't think anyone doubts that. Recently, however, speculation has revived once again that Bergoglio might be considering imposing restrictions of some kind on its celebration. This fear has been prompted by the circulation by the Vatican to the world's bishops of a tendentious questionnaire on the status of the celebration of the Old Mass. Also, certain bureaucratic moves and restructurings (e.g., the abolition of the *Ecclesiae Dei* commission) in the Vatican led some to think that a clique adverse to traditionalism is consolidating its power. Curiously, some of the more recent developments took place after the release by the Vatican of optional new prefaces and saints' commemorations for the Old Mass—a move seen at least by outraged progressives as an unacceptable acknowledgment of that Mass's continued vitality.

One might puzzle over the timing of such a hypothetical papal intervention. For the state of the Church and of the Vatican under Pope Francis is anything but good. As we have set forth above, regardless of what anyone is publicly saying, the Church will not emerge unscathed from coronavirus. Numerous Vatican scandals continue to seethe. All objective statistics regarding Mass attendance, reception of the sacraments, vocations, etc. show a Church in catastrophic retreat across the world. Concerns are mounting over the German "synodal path," an initiative, after all, originally instigated by Francis, with worldwide ramifications. And the tensions over Francis's "Amazonian" synod triggered not very well disguised opposition

---

2   This of course was before the imposition of any restrictions under *Traditionis Custodes*!

in the form of essays written by Cardinal Sarah and, more importantly, the "pope emeritus." I would be very surprised if those essays hadn't played a role in temporarily putting the brakes on the seemingly triumphal progress toward married priests and women clergy.

It would not seem a propitious moment to set off an ecclesiastical civil war. But, as I wrote in 2014, a moment like today, where Francis is confronting setbacks on other fronts, would likely be the perfect occasion to launch an attack on traditionalists. For, in addition to distracting from his other difficulties, such a move would certainly win the applause of most hierarchies and ecclesiastical bureaucracies—especially those of Europe—as well as of the secular media. But will it happen? Possibly, but the traditionalist movement has had to live over the years with various threats from the Vatican, both known and not so well known, and by the grace of God has thus far survived them.

Yet what will be the outcome of all this? Will traditionalism survive only as a Roman Catholic version of Anglo-Catholicism? Does not Pope Francis himself increasingly give the Church an "Anglican" face: a bureaucratic superstructure entirely focused on the secular, devoid of any specific spiritual and moral content, but to some extent tolerating the existence of "minorities"—the African churches, the traditionalists—still loyal to a different and older morality, liturgy, and theology? If so, it would be a tragic and futile conclusion of a sixty-year struggle.

At times the temptation has indeed been great for traditionalists to play the role of "High Church Catholicism": preserving the traditional Mass, often presented as a special event, but otherwise quietly accepting the present state of the Roman Catholic Church and of that of the society to which the Church in turn has conformed. Such traditionalists, going beyond requisite and commendable prudence, have restrained their commentary on the pressing issues of the day. They have at times practiced self-censorship as the price of admission to the churches and institutions owned by the establishment.

But, by its very nature, the traditional Mass rejects confinement within such a straitjacket. This liturgy can never be a private option or merely a psychologically beneficial ritual. By constantly recalling and representing the presence and active role of God, by making visible and vital once more the riches of art and history and by insisting on the role of reason, the traditional Mass can never be a pliant servant of modernity. This Mass leads souls to contemplation, yet paradoxically—or not?—inspires them to external works, setting off shock waves in art, politics, and ecclesiastical life. Do we not see this in the "direct action" of Alexander Tschugguel (tossing Pachamama in the Tiber) in response to the "enthronement" of a fake but highly symbolic idol in the Vatican? Or in the continuing active participation of Latin Mass congregations in the US pro-life movement? Or in the apostolic voyages of men such as Cardinal Burke, Cardinal Zen, or Bishop Athanasius Schneider, who take uncompromising public stands on the crucial issues of Church and society, regardless of the popularity of these opinions? Or even in the transition of one prominent traditionalist blog (*Rorate Caeli*) from the futility of covering the day-to-day nonsense of today's Church to a more immediately relevant, unapologetic advocacy for Donald Trump?

It is now the time to advocate openly for Catholic truth in liturgy, morality, and theology. As we have said, this may well lead in the short term to conflict—even a dramatic showdown—with the forces controlling the Catholic institutions. But to shirk this confrontation will mean only to involve traditionalism in the overall collapse of the Catholic establishment. After this crisis, traditional Catholics will need to work ever more diligently and learn to cooperate closely among themselves—despite the recent difficulties. They will need to continue supporting the prayer of the contemplative monasticism of the Benedictines in Norcia, Italy; Silverstream, Ireland; Clear Creek, Oklahoma; and the Benedictines of Mary, Queen of Apostles, in Missouri; the Carmelite Monks in Wyoming, and the many houses of cloistered traditional Carmelite nuns; and other communities like these. They will likewise need to sponsor the work of Catholic scholars, writers, and intellectuals. They must maintain the commitment to liturgical excellence and completeness which happily has been so widely achieved today. And they will continue to foster vocations as priests and religious.

They cannot shy away from the conflicts that will inevitably arise with a disintegrating hierarchy and secular society. They must take in stride being called mentally ill (Pope Francis), repressed homosexuals (Frederic Martel), "enemies of the Pope" (the establishment Catholic news media) and, of course, "fascists" (everywhere in Europe), and know that it cannot be otherwise. As Pope Benedict so bitterly experienced, the post-Conciliar old order will not go down without a savage fight. It will be a struggle in which the opponents of Catholic Tradition will continue to enjoy the full support of the secular world. Yet when they look at the numbers, traditionalists are increasingly confident that the future is on their side, regardless of whatever drastic challenges the immediate future may bring. And for the vital majority, the scope of their mission is no longer, as in 1970, "saving the Mass" for a few, but restoring integral Catholic Tradition in all its glory to the whole Church.

8 A Bumpy Ride for Traditionalists

2021

SINCE THE START OF 2021 OVERT ATTACKS on traditionalism have multiplied. Recall the entirely negative "Summary" of the French bishops' reports[1] on *Summorum Pontificum*, Bishop Robert Barron's diatribe against "fierce" traditionalists,[2] and most recently the attacks by Thomas Reese SJ suggesting that the use of the traditional Mass be banned outright.[3] What is noteworthy is that all these assaults were launched by prominent members of the Catholic administrative or media establishment. Furthermore, these critics of Catholic traditionalism enjoy other significant connections. Thomas Reese's contribution, for example, was first published in Religious News Service (RNS), a secular platform for officially approved views to be disseminated by the mainstream media. And Reese made his remarks on the old Mass in the context of other recommendations very much aligned

---

1   https://fsspx.news/sites/sspx/files/202012synthesecefsummorum-pontificium.pdf.

2   https://www.wordonfire.org/resources/article/the-evangelical-path-of-word-on-fire/30079/.

3   "The future of Catholic liturgical reform," *Religion News Service*, April 13, 2021.

with the objectives of the Synodal Path in Germany (such
as female clergy).

Now some on the right chose to ignore these statements
or questioned their legal significance. I think this is very
short-sighted. Catholic bishops and especially Jesuit priests
hardly ever make statements out of a disinterested love of
truth. These comments would never have been made if
the authors had not been sure of an at least benevolent
reception on the part of both their colleagues and in
Rome. I might be missing something, but I don't recall
reading any statements in support of *Summorum Pontificum* or traditionalism from similarly situated sources in
the hierarchy or Catholic media.

Let us look at these comments and try to synthesize them.
In so doing I hope I am not being unfair: the liturgical ideas
of Thomas Reese and those of Bishop Barron are not exactly
the same. I do not intend to focus on the contradictions and
preposterous assertions of the three "indictments"—which
are evident on the face of these documents. Rather, I would
like to consider not so much what the authors are saying
about Catholic traditionalism but what they are saying about
themselves. What do we learn about the features of the Catholic Church in 2021 from these various "position papers"?

First, this Church is *authoritarian*. Bishop Barron is concerned about opposition to the Council and to the Pope. No
attempt is made to make the case for either, or to convince
opponents—the immunity of Council and Pope from criticism is presupposed. Similarly, the French bishops' Summary takes the existing liturgical establishment in France
as a given not needing any further defense or explication.
Unquestioning loyalty to the existing "system" and to the
ecclesiastical authorities is expected.

Second, in the understanding of especially Reese *the liturgy is a created thing, an administrative product.* It is something

that can be altered or abolished at the will of the clergy. This understanding is in stark contrast to Joseph Ratzinger's initial horror over the Novus Ordo introduction in 1969 which he saw as destroying the notion of the liturgy as something pre-existing for us, not created by us. Of course, *Summorum Pontificum*, reflecting these insights, defined the old liturgy as something that could not be abolished. Certainly the understanding of the Eastern Orthodox is very similar.

Third, *unity is posited as an absolute value*. The Summary of the French bishops obsessively emphasizes the danger of disunity: the horrors of different liturgical calendars, different liturgies, different ecclesial understandings, etc. Bishop Barron sees himself as part of a great center set off against "beige Catholics" on the one hand and traditionalists on the other.

Fourth, the Church of Reese, Barron, and the French bishops' Summary is *lawless*. Thomas Reese feels empowered by the Council to disregard not just *Summorum Pontificum* but also *Ecclesia Dei* and much other legislation authorizing the traditional rite. And what precedent is there for a rule excluding persons below a certain age from attending a rite of the Church? The French bishops' Summary does the same: "The FSSP, by celebrating exclusively in the extraordinary form, poses a problem for diocesan life and this practice is contrary to the sense of the Motu Proprio" (without citing any authority for this assertion). Do not these authors, however, have the best of authority in the practices of Pope Francis, who has systematically disregarded customs, canon law, and liturgical rules from the beginning of his pontificate? Only in the last few months, for example, we have seen Francis impose restrictions on the celebration of the Mass, including the traditional Mass, in Saint Peter's in Rome, disregarding all procedural and substantive church law.

Fifth, Reese, Barron, and the French bishops are *contemptuous of those who may deviate from the "party line"* and of their motivations.

- Reese: "The church needs to be clear that it wants the unreformed liturgy to disappear and will only allow it out of pastoral kindness to older people who do not understand the need for change."
- The French Summary: "For many of the faithful worshipping in the extraordinary form the Christian life consists of Sunday attendance without any other spiritual or theological formation. We are far from Pope Francis's conception of a missionary disciple."
- Barron: "These arch-traditionalist Catholics have become nostalgic for the Church of the preconciliar period."

There is no possibility of dialogue here. No attempt is made to actually "engage" with these problematic traditionalists to understand what they're thinking, let alone reach an accommodation with them. The pre-*Summorum Pontificum* indults were promulgated based on the alleged concern of the Church for those "attached to" the traditional Mass—such considerations don't seem to play a role anymore.

None of this is new. The understanding of the liturgy (and its artistic and cultural appurtenances) as an arbitrary clerical creation, the authoritarianism, the brusque disregard of legal formalities and of the rights of all those holding other views, the goal of a quasi-totalitarian unity, the aggressive and hostile attitude towards conservative "dissidents"—these things have dominated since the very beginning of the conciliar era. To illustrate, I recall that at Georgetown University around 1973 the Jesuit liturgists were insisting on a radical reconstruction of the university chapel—which they of course eventually achieved. But initially, substantial opposition was led, I recall, by a member of the arts faculty. The Jesuit leading the charge for "reform" informed those assembled at a "town meeting" that, after all, he didn't care how many opposed his plans or why—it was the liturgical thing to do and he would force it through. Need I mention that it was an aesthetic disaster and that it all had to be redone within a few years?

Our authors' contributions reveal to us a Church that is fossilized. The same clichés are repeated over and over just as they were in the 1960s:

- that traditionalists are old nostalgic people (Reese);
- that the establishment stands in the center between extremes (Barron);
- that we need more and more Eucharistic prayers (Reese again).

As an aside, in the 1970s, didn't the Catholic chaplaincy at Cornell University offer a book with 50 or so (unauthorized) canons?

Obviously the "Council" means a set of assumptions and rules—an ideology—that has become fixed and unchangeable.

Martin Mosebach, in an interview in 2019, enraged the "German Church" when he compared the public appearances of Pope Francis with those of Stalin or Hitler. Yet recently I've been reading that the late Hans Küng seems to have repeatedly compared the Catholic Church with the Soviet Union. I think Küng was far more prescient then he ever realized. Because the Church establishment—in its fanatical, uncompromising insistence on immutable positions which can never be controverted by any appeal to the facts—is entirely in line with the *modus operandi* of the Soviet party bureaucracy in its last decades.

What will be the result of these efforts against tradition-alism? I do not know! Pope Francis, of course, could very well impose restrictions of some kind on the celebration of the traditional Mass and thereby score some easy points with the Church establishment—especially the European hierarchies and the major religious orders everywhere. It would, however, seem odd for the Pope to move on this front eight years into his pontificate—especially with Pope Benedict still alive. And given the developments in traditionalism since the promulgation of *Summorum Pontificum*, I do not know how many traditionalists would follow him at this stage. And, after all, there is a minority tendency among progressives that tolerates the traditional Mass (think of Bernardin!).

Moreover, I think our enemies are talking from a posi-tion of weakness, not strength. Pope Francis recently has been forced to adopt an ambiguous position on sev-eral issues—married priests, women deacons, "synodal-ity"—because of the German Synodal Path (which he himself, of course, helped to launch) and opposition, both overt and behind the scenes, elsewhere in the Church. Those who would wish to restrict or even outlaw the traditional Mass may see this as their last chance in this pontificate before Francis dies or some new destabilizing scandal in the Church or the Vatican erupts. Before the ever-accelerating decline of Mass attendance, vocations, and monetary support by the laity reaches catastrophic proportions. The rediscovered rage against traditionalists may be only the establishment's last gasp of despair.

9 American Catholic Traditionalism in 2021

I

T IS EIGHT YEARS INTO THE PONTIFICATE OF Pope Francis. I would like to take stock once again of where American Catholic traditionalism stands. But before dealing with traditionalism, I need to set the stage by outlining the historical situation in which we find ourselves. Why? Because the Catholic traditionalist movement does not exist in a vacuum. It is situated—especially after *Summorum Pontificum*—in the greater Catholic Church, both of the United States and of the world. And that Catholic Church finds itself in a specific historical context.

Speaking of the larger society, the United States-led Western world has undeniably reached a crossroads. The turmoil of the last few years has scarred the country: the coronavirus shock, the political agitation and violence on the streets, and five years of virtual civil war between President Donald Trump and the American establishment. Within the United States, the forces of the establishment— the so-called deep state, civil society or "power elite"—have shifted easily into an overtly totalitarian mode of operation. In the wake of the coronavirus, the government assumed the right to regulate the most intimate details of the life of its citizens even within the walls of their own homes. Throughout the educational system and business enterprises those who merely refrained from endorsing—let alone challenged or questioned—the emerging orthodoxies were blacklisted and suspended or fired from their positions. And all too often the victims then confessed their culpability themselves, very much in the style of the Moscow show trials. Censorship of social media has become virtually official practice. Finally, we witnessed the *Reichstag Fire* of January's events on Capitol Hill.

During all of this, Americans—or rather a large percentage of them—were gripped by a rising tide of fear and hysteria, fostered by the news media. People are afraid of many things; the coronavirus, domestic violence and disorders, economic disaster. One sees this in the fearful actions of those hiding because of the risk of contagion or who grow confrontational regarding preserving social distance or wearing a mask. The Biden presidency was in part sold on the deceptive promise of a return to normalcy. We are already seeing how unlikely that's going to be—just on the international front, fresh crises are already forming. The American establishment has prevailed so far, yet its triumphs already seem like a pyrrhic victory.

The traditional American Catholic has become in many respects the proverbial *man without a country*. The United States, where his parents and grandparents were so happy to "fit in," now describes itself as "systemically racist." The institutions that this Catholic "man in the street" had been taught to revere, rightly or wrongly—like the great universities, the military, the major corporations, the police—are all now completely indifferent if not downright hostile to him. Moreover, is he not told frequently that his Christian faith itself is a problem?—witness the fate of previously revered monuments to Catholic heroes or the ongoing campaign to purge every reference to Christianity from the public discourse. The governing progressive powers remain militantly opposed to all the social and moral doctrines that the Church had previously encouraged the laity to advocate "in the public square." But, marginalized by secular society, the Catholic finds his home in his own Church crumbling as well. In the coronavirus panic, the Catholic laity have been restricted or prohibited from attending Mass, receiving the sacraments, and even stopping into church for prayer. Indeed, the laity had been largely dispensed from any requirements associated with these practices anyway.

This exclusion of Catholics from the new American mainstream of course also applies to the institutional Church as well. The Catholic Church has performed abysmally in these trying times. The bishops have accepted without protest the closing of their churches and schools, the suspension of the sacraments, the reduction of Catholic life to a primarily "virtual" affair. The bishops and clergy have even at times exceeded the requirements of the state. At no time in the past have the bishops imposed rules regarding the liturgy as stringent—and drastically enforced—as the lockdown regulations they universally enacted. In the face of the rise in political violence, the bishops sought to straddle the fence, cautiously endorsing protesters who overthrew statues of Catholic heroes of yore like Columbus or Junípero Serra.

Meanwhile, the crisis generated by the sexual abuse scandals—with its adverse press coverage, financial damage, and diocesan bankruptcies—continues to fester with no end in sight. The same is true for the endless series of closings of parishes, schools, and seminaries. The Church continues to be unable to recruit sufficient priests, brothers, and sisters to maintain its institutional presence. The impact of the

Catholic Church on public policy, thought, and culture is nonexistent—unless, of course, like Pope Francis, it is endorsing the agenda of the secular establishment.

The culmination of all these trends is the coronation by the media of President Joe Biden as a "devout" Catholic—seemingly *because* he has so explicitly rejected non-negotiable moral positions of the Catholic Church. While President Biden continues to implement his stated commitment in support of abortion, the American bishops have not yet been able to formulate any response. The Vatican and the Pope's most obsequious followers among the American bishops are actively working to block or delay any attempt to draw consequences from the conflict between Biden's agenda and the principles the bishops had previously advocated (at least, in the case of most of them, on paper). This futility in dealing with such a prominent issue only confirms once again the lack of leadership, the conformism, and the pusillanimity of establishment Catholicism in the United States.

The result of all this is most likely an accelerating disassociation of the laity from the institutional Church. Estimates indicate that, once the coronavirus restrictions end, a substantial part of the laity may never return to the public practice of the faith. That threatens to be life-threatening for the American Church, given that the continued vitality—and funding—of American Catholicism rests largely on habits of conformity inherited ultimately from the preconciliar era.

In contrast to prior decades there is no possibility of turning to Rome. For the pope is as committed to the secular agenda of the Western establishment as the most radical American Catholic progressives. He has assumed—at least in appearance—an attitude of indifference to "life issues" and has expressed disdain for "culture warriors." But

Francis's own situation is not good. A cult of personality around Francis continues to be fostered without generating any real support in popular sentiment. Continued scandals in the Vatican, aggressive progressive agitation (especially in Germany), and ever-increasing financial difficulties foretell a dire future for the central administration of the Church. Meanwhile, the unending stream of actions and statements of the pope in areas such as marriage, homo-sexuality, environmentalism, and secular politics will, in the long term, undoubtedly undermine the credibility of the Catholic Church as a spiritual force.

Does it not seem like an eerie return of the political and ecclesiastical chaos of the 1960s? The *immediate* prac-tical effects on the life of the American Church, however, could not be more different. In many respects, Francis has simply ratified existing practices or abuses, not bro-ken new ground. At least in the New York area, only the growing official recognition of the LGBT movement by the New York archdiocese represents a new, post-Francis development. Unlike his predecessor 55 years ago, Francis has not set off a revolutionary destructive wave within parishes, religious orders, and educational institutions. To some extent, of course, this is because those institutions have by now been largely destroyed or secularized. We could also say that the earlier reverence for the central-ized authority of the Church among the laity has largely dissipated. In fact, those forces that Francis scorns—the pro-life movement, the Catholic conservatives,[1] and of course the traditionalists—have largely continued on their accustomed path regardless of either what the Pope says or what is happening in secular politics.

---

1 For a discussion of the term "Catholic Conservatism," as opposed to the clerical establishment on the one hand and Tra-ditionalism on the other, see Chapter 2.

For Catholic conservatism the era of Francis—now merging with the age of Biden—has been particularly traumatic. For the Catholic hierarchy has all but officially adopted the seamless garment ideology crafted by the Catholic progressives years ago and so disputed by the conservatives. The progressive forces themselves now go much further and border on expressly advocating the complete abandonment of the pro-life cause.

No faction within Catholicism set as much store on the papacy as did the Catholic conservatives. And now this same papacy has explicitly rejected everything the Catholic conservatives stood for: the political alliance with Evangelicals, abortion as a paramount issue, the defense of capitalism, and the support of American intervention throughout the world. Furthermore it is very clear that attempts to cooperate with the hierarchy in revitalizing Catholicism in seminaries and parishes are making little or no progress. The favored organizational form of conservative Catholic apostolates—an unstructured "movement" dominated by a charismatic authoritarian figure—has also led again and again to embarrassment and failure.

Yet the reaction of the Catholic conservatives, except in some rare cases, has not been to go over to the camp of the enemy. They may have been abandoned by the Pope and disappointed by the lukewarmness of the Catholic hierarchy but they will not, just because of this, abandon their pro-life positions or their other historic causes. The pro-life movement, for example, remains active and continues its political advocacy, most often working with political leaders aligned with the Trump, populist wing of the Republican party.

Many of the most outspoken representatives of conservative Catholicism were unable to repudiate their principles and jump on the Francis bandwagon. They have developed into outspoken critics of one or another aspect of the Catholic Church today. This resilience in the face of papal and hierarchical indifference or hostility is largely due to the greatly expanded network of Catholic media—especially social media. There is a vast array of sources—mostly online—available for those who wish to inform themselves better about the Church today. We could mention, among others, the *Catholic News Agency*, the *National Catholic Register*, *LifeSiteNews*, the new *Pillar. com*, *Crisis*, and *Catholic Culture*, as well as a whole army of blogs. Finally, going beyond reporting and commenting on daily events, there is the revitalized *First Things* which has moved away from its original neoconservative ideology. All of this makes available to the Catholic who wants it a mass of information and articulate, critical commentary. We can understand the fury of the advocates of Francis confronted by this new reality and their constant talk about regulating or censoring the Catholic online presence.

The conservative Catholics have redoubled their commitment to creating new practical apostolates—which, after all, has always been the thing they do best. The actions of FOCUS and certain other Catholic campus ministries are one of the few bright spots in today's Church—an amazing contrast to the dreadful situation prevailing on campuses in the 1970s and 1980s. A new Catholic residential community is organizing in Texas, resembling Ave Maria Village in Florida—even if its structure features a superabundance of apostolic organizations in relation to its size. Surprisingly, even in secular academia advocates for Catholicism are standing up. We have the intellectual movement of integralism dealing with Catholic concepts of Church/State relations—led by, among others, a professor at Harvard and a Cistercian monk. More recently, a society dedicated to reexamining and recovering Catholic

philosophy is forming at Princeton University. An organization has been launched seeking to develop authors
to revitalize Catholic literature. Once again, after several
false starts, another attempt is being made to create a
national Catholic magazine: *The Lamp*. The initiatives
on the musical front are too numerous to describe here.
Finally, just in my immediate neighborhood, three major
new "conservative" Catholic (using that term somewhat
loosely) schools are in the process of formation (joining
one already existing independent Catholic classical school).
This is in the diocese of Bridgeport, Connecticut, where
just sixteen years ago no school of this kind existed at all.

Now I might very well have critical comments on aspects
of these initiatives. As always among conservative Catholics,
moreover, not all these groups are aligned. To some extent,
the temptation remains of substituting apostolic activity
for spiritual development—or of utilizing it to avoid facing
reality. Yet the continued vitality of the "orthodox" wing of
Catholicism—largely supported by the laity on a voluntary
basis—cannot be denied. And we are also happy to note
that some—certainly not all—of these initiatives are open
to cooperation with traditionalists. The self-understanding
of conservative Catholicism as the "Uniate" alternative to
traditionalism is steadily eroding.

II

IN THIS AGE OF RESURGENT REVOLUTION, LIQUI-
fying institutions, and mounting fears, traditional Catholicism has not fallen apart, but has continued to advance.
This fact is no longer just an assertion by traditionalists. The
flourishing of traditionalist life in the years since *Summorum
Pontificum* has been noted with fear and rage—especially
by the official Catholic media and the European clergy.

The new traditionalist generation is indeed young and to a great extent includes growing families. And a new young generation of priest leaders has grown up as well. But what is really distinctive of traditionalism today is that it is lived out in "stable groups of the faithful"—as mentioned in *Summorum Pontificum* itself. Specifically in the United States, we have witnessed the emergence of fully-formed *Summorum Pontificum* parish life. And in contrast to the Indult regime—and the normal Novus Ordo parish, I should add—these communities now have an outward, not inward, focus.

We have seen that American traditionalism emerged from the "underground" in the United States after the Indults of 1984/1988. Traditionalism since 1969 (and really since 1964) had until then remained the one group within Catholicism that was officially and relentlessly persecuted. Its adherents had lived in small groups or in isolation. This is true both for those who frequented FSSPX chapels, those who attended the Masses of independent priests, and those who followed traditionalism more by reading about it. Of necessity, the traditionalist community featured a great degree of individuality, not to say at times eccentricity and even dogmatism in questions of the faith and the liturgy. It was also true that the core of the traditionalists at that time had known the old Mass prior to the Council.

After the Indults, traditionalists organized and formed groups to support the new Masses they were permitted to celebrate. In their new freedom and visibility they had to face a wide variety of issues they did not have to deal with in their prior existence as an underground resistance. For example, traditionalists had to pay much more attention to the aesthetic aspect of their Masses. In some places greater care—almost unprecedented within the American Catholic Church in the previous decades—was now taken with music. I am thinking of the (still existing) St. Gregory Society of New Haven. And as the number of Masses celebrated in the United States increased, the number of new adherents increased as well, drawn from those who previously had never experienced the traditional liturgy. A new generation was gradually taking over and transforming traditionalism.

This demographic development was evident to me in the membership of the American contingent at the Chartres "Pilgrimage of Christendom" between the early 1990s and 2010. On the first pilgrimage in which I participated, the rather mature age (including my own!) of most of the American pilgrims was striking compared to that of the scouts who made up the bulk of the French contingents. Yet by 2010 that had changed—the American pilgrims were, on the whole, of the same average (youthful!) age as their European counterparts.

From 2007 onward, *Summorum Pontificum* greatly accelerated these tendencies. The drastic restrictions of the Indult regime began to loosen. In many parish churches a traditionalist community "moved in" as a new neighbor, the subject of continued distancing but also of curiosity. Previously existing independent chapels or venues for solitary indult Masses were absorbed and transformed by the new movement. Traditionalism also no longer meant celebrating just one Sunday Mass but providing all the sacraments in the traditional form. As the number of Masses expanded, the congregations grew as well, as did the number of priests who wanted to celebrate the traditional rite.

The result, in the most successful traditionalist apostolates, was the appearance of the revived traditionalist parish. Such a parish regularly celebrates the Solemn High Mass—or at least a *Missa Cantata*—on Sundays and major feast days. The community celebrates all the sacraments in the traditional rite. A good number of young men volunteer to serve at the altar—indeed, as in the "good old days," scheduling is necessary. Music achieves an increasingly professional level—the vestments, decoration of the altar, and other artwork complement the level of the music. I have heard tell that one well-known traditionalist, recently deceased, had finally decided to become a Catholic just because of his new experience of singing chant in a *Summorum Pontificum* parish. And there is a constant striving for perfection of the liturgy. The celebration of the pre-1955 Holy Week liturgies or the use of the folded chasuble were the province of a liturgical avant-garde ten years ago—now these practices are widespread and almost routine.

The consequences are quick to follow. From the ranks of the altar servers come vocations to the priesthood. The congregation continues to expand because of that unfailing rule: Catholic traditionalism grows only by individual exposure to the old Mass. And in these expanded congregations social events—coffee hours, receptions, dinners, fundraising affairs—spontaneously spring up, linking the members of the community outside of liturgical celebrations. The contrast is astonishing between such a parish and even the most successful pre-2007 Indult groups.

Naturally I am describing a minority of exemplary communities. For much of American traditionalism, life still revolves around a single Sunday Mass attended by a small congregation. And many groups still cannot obtain even a regular Mass on Sunday. In a small, originally Italian parish not too far from where I live, a Saturday morning Mass has been started by a priest ordained six years ago. But as often as is humanly possible, his Saturday Mass is a *Missa Cantata*, celebrated with all the propers chanted in full. That's more than could be found in most of the well-attended High Masses of the preconciliar days. The overall tendency is clear!

A great "penumbra" of traditionalist life has also arisen outside of the totally committed traditionalist communities. In the *Summorum Pontificum* world, traditionalists most often share a parish with other communities and rites. A fruitful interaction can result on this level—I have seen amazing combinations of the traditional Liturgy with the Holy Week processions and other customs of Latin American Catholics. Some parishes celebrate a festive traditional Mass only on special occasions and holy days. Many grand churches otherwise not at all involved in the traditionalist cause have opened their doors to an occasional traditional liturgy. In New York, for example, St. Patrick's Cathedral (both old and new), St. Vincent Ferrer, Blessed Sacrament, St. Jean Baptiste... At least in our part of the country, quite a few bishops (and several visiting cardinals) celebrate the traditional Mass. And the reach of traditionalism is even greater than this. The *Rorate* Mass, an Advent liturgy celebrated in the darkness of early dawn, was revived not that long ago by traditionalists. This custom has now spread to the Novus Ordo as well.

Now what are the traditionalists' principles? Obviously first and foremost is the celebration of the traditional liturgy that has become the non-negotiable hallmark of traditionalist Catholicism. But Catholic traditionalists are in no way some kind of "papal" Anglo-Catholics. After all, the traditionalist devotion to the Old Mass had to function for decades without the benefit of the—admittedly highly desirable—aesthetic features so essential to conservative Episcopalians. The celebration of the liturgy for traditionalists, moreover, has been inseparable from full adherence to the theology and morality as expressed by Catholic tradition. From its very inception in the 1960s the traditionalist movement made a forceful critique of the policies emerging from the Second Vatican Council: ecumenism, obsessive focus on dialogue, loss or denial of Catholic uniqueness, a conciliatory attitude to communism and leftism, and toleration if not downright approval of moral deviations of every kind.

For the same reason, a traditionalist community—even the most institutional, "normalized" examples—can never be just a Novus Ordo parish with the traditional liturgy, let alone a revival of its preconciliar predecessor. There is an interest and commitment to the intellectual, liturgical, and moral questions of the day among the traditionalists that sets them apart from their fellow Catholics. Not that traditionalist congregations are dominated by debates about theology, morality, or the latest course the Vatican is taking—quite the contrary. Surveys have indicated, however, that among traditionalist Catholics can be found higher level of knowledge of the Catholic faith—and certainly greater adherence to Catholic morality and the precepts of the Church.

It has been rightly pointed out that part of the reason for this American success story is the greater willingness of individual Catholics—both in the priesthood and among the laity—to take the initiative and work together to achieve objectives. For to this day there is no organization, religious congregation, or publication providing centralized leadership and direction to the American traditionalists. This does not mean that all traditionalist Catholics have come to agree among themselves on all points—far from it. Yet they are mostly—not always—able to surmount those differences to cooperate for a supremely worthwhile cause.

The current American traditionalist success story, of course, is also based on the fact that the same sense of pragmatism can be found among much of the American

hierarchy. The average American bishop cannot afford to
be as totally indifferent to Mass attendance, public relations, or the morale of the laity in his diocese as are his
European counterparts or the bureaucrats of the Vatican.
From very early on, if only as a question of pragmatism,
many bishops have shown themselves more or less willing
to work with traditionalists. Some have gone much further
than that. We have experienced how bishops in our region
repeatedly have intervened directly to remove obstacles to
the traditional liturgy raised by local pastors. They have
permitted traditional liturgies in their own cathedrals
and in other major shrines and basilicas. Now and then
a favorable mention of traditionalism even appears in
the official diocesan press (*mirabile dictu!*). It would be a
mistake, therefore, to view the relationship between the
hierarchy and traditionalism as uniformly hostile—at least,
I should repeat, in the New York area.

On the other hand, these same local ordinaries by no
stretch of the imagination foster or encourage the spread
of traditionalism. Rather, in actual practice an arbitrarily
enforced, restrictive policy of control prevails (especially
as to the clergy). In some respects very little has changed
from the Indult regime. As a matter of routine, traditionalist priests are still summarily transferred from parishes
and "exiled" to less attractive—and certainly far less visible—positions. For the local traditionalist community that
can mean termination of their liturgies if no like-minded
successor is provided. The increasing number of young
priests who choose traditionalism make an especially great
sacrifice. As one traditionalist priest recently said, there
is no surer way of destroying your ecclesiastical career
than declaring yourself in favor of the Old Mass. Other
diocesan employees are similarly fearful of advertising
traditionalist sympathies.

This bias is also reflected in the allocation of diocesan resources. Traditionalists were entranced in 2020, for example, by a festive liturgy and conference that took place at St. Vincent Ferrer church in New York City. And that was organized and funded by traditionalists without direct support of the Archdiocese. Yet, on that very same weekend, the Archdiocese of New York sponsored a three-day extravaganza with Communion and Liberation (the Italian "movement" originally aimed at students) featuring speakers, prelates, and performers from all over the country. I think it is fair to say that Communion and Liberation has only a tiny fraction of the resonance that the traditionalist movement enjoys either in the Archdiocese of New York or nationwide.

III

SUCH IS THE ORDINARY LIFE OF AMERICAN TRA-
ditionalism today: organizing Masses; establishing chapels, parishes, and schools; finally, if possible, participating in conferences, public processions, and pilgrimages, both in and outside of the United States. I had written in 2014, however, that to continue its progress, American traditionalism needed to find its own saints and scholars—just as Europe did in the age of St. Patrick, St. Benedict, St. Boniface and so many others, when the Church converted both the disintegrating Roman world and the new barbarian nations.

In 2021 that need is even more dire. The great number of younger people newly introduced to traditionalism require liturgical, theological, and historical instruction. Further, traditionalists are compelled to explain and justify (as in the apologias for Christianity in pagan Roman times) their beliefs to an often hostile outside world. Finally, traditionalism must develop a deeper understanding of its own origins and of how the Catholic Church got to the

position it is in today. What is the intellectual and spiritual
life of the traditionalists—and what leaders have emerged?

I should start with the active, apostolic fraternities of
priests, beginning with the Priestly Society of St. Pius X
(FSSPX) founded by Archbishop Marcel Lefebvre. The
FSSPX initiated the rebirth of the practice of traditional
Catholicism, both internationally and in the United States.
The Fraternity has continued its steady progress in the
last eight years. In many respects a *modus vivendi* has been
achieved with the Vatican, so the voices in America who
continue to denounce the alleged schismatics have receded
into the background. A grand new seminary was inaugurated five years ago in the state of Virginia to accommodate
the growing number of young seminarians. The Fraternity
also maintains its own chapels, schools, and publications.
On the other hand, the FSSPX has not taken a leading
role in the debates on the Church and the world of the
present day. Perhaps this more cautious public face is due
to another schism within the Fraternity—that involving
Bishop Williamson, which resulted in the formation within
North America of the "SSPX—Marian Corps" (aka the
"Resistance" or the "Strict Observance"). Perhaps it reflects
continued fond hopes of obtaining a more regular status
from the Vatican.

The Priestly Fraternity of St. Peter (FSSP), an offspring
of the FSSPX originating in resistance to Archbishop
Lefebvre's 1988 episcopal consecrations, also continues
to make steady progress. I am told that their seminary,
completed only in 2010, already cannot accommodate all
the candidates. The FSSP principally staffs a network of
parishes throughout the United States. I have otherwise
heard very little from the Fraternity recently—quite a
contrast with its prominence among traditionalists in the
decade after the 1988 Indult.

Recently, however, the most active of these priestly societies has been the Institute of Christ the King Sovereign Priest (ICRSS or ICKSP). It perhaps has understood best the new opportunities available to traditionalists under *Summorum Pontificum.* Noteworthy is their outward, evangelical focus and a certain—shall we say—showmanship? The ICRSS, for example, pays close attention to the aesthetic details of the liturgy. It also specializes in taking over and restoring magnificent old churches abandoned by their dioceses because a loss of the congregation or the parish's "bad neighborhood."

Just in the last several years the Institute has made major inroads in Connecticut. In Waterbury (Hartford archdiocese) the ICRSS assumed the administration of the grand church of St. Patrick with enigmatic Irish-language inscriptions on the stained glass windows. In so doing, they have built upon and continued the celebration of the Latin Mass in that city—a tradition that in one form or another stretches back to 2007 and before. At almost the same time, the ICRSS took over a second church, Sts. Cyril and Methodius in Bridgeport (Bridgeport Diocese). An old Slovak church, Sts. Cyril and Methodius is situated in the midst of a virtual moonscape emblematic of American industrial and urban decay. But the church had been lovingly preserved by its long-term pastor who for decades celebrated an Indult Mass there for a small congregation. The Institute, building on these foundations, has awakened the parish to vigorous new life.

Yet perhaps the most heartening development is the resurgence of traditionalist contemplative life. Has not the priority given historically to action over contemplation been a glaring defect not only of American Catholicism but of post-1830 ultramontane Catholicism in general? We might start our survey with the flourishing Clear

Creek Abbey in Oklahoma (Our Lady of Clear Creek)
which has been in existence since 1999—back then I met
on a transatlantic flight two monks returning to France
from scouting out the location of the new monastery! An
abbey since 2010, Clear Creek now has 50 monks and is
engaged in a major building campaign. I have heard of
families moving to that area in order to regularly attend
the abbey's services.

Also representative are the Carmelite Monks of the
Most Blessed Virgin Mary of Mount Carmel of Wyoming.
These are cloistered contemplative monks, not mendicant
friars. As to their liturgy, they state:

> According to the Motu Proprio *Summorum Pon-
> tificum* of His Holiness Pope Benedict XVI, and
> the corresponding Instruction *Universae Ecclesiae*,
> the Monks of the Most Blessed Virgin Mary
> of Mount Carmel have unanimously chosen to
> permanently retain the Carmelite Rite as the Lit-
> urgy of their institute according to the Carmelite
> liturgical books in use in 1962.

This monastery is also widely known for the brand of
coffee it sells to support itself!

Of the female orders, perhaps the best known are the
Benedictines of Mary, Queen of the Apostles in Gower
Missouri. In 2018 the monastery was raised to an abbey
and a new abbey church was consecrated. The ceremony
for the consecration of their abbess, unique up till now in
the United States, attracted wide attention. This monastery
is also well known outside of just Catholic circles for its
acclaimed, best-selling recordings of chant. Mention should
also be made of a number of communities of Discalced
Carmelites.

But two monasteries, located outside the United States
but having many American members, have had perhaps

the greatest resonance. Silverstream Priory in Ireland was founded in 2012 by Americans and erected as a monastery of diocesan right in 2017. The monks are widely known for their distribution of literature—some written by themselves—and for their dedication to Eucharistic adoration and reparation on behalf of the clergy.

The traditional monastery of San Benedetto in Monte of Norcia, Italy, has achieved world fame. Their beer, Birra Nursia, has acquired a great reputation on these shores. Then there's the heroic saga of the monks' recovery, with the help of international donations, from the earthquake which destroyed their previous monastery. Their campaign to build a new monastery is ongoing. The greatest notoriety was achieved, however, by the publication of Rod Dreher's *Benedict Option* in 2017. The Norcia monks appear there as a model of a Christian community cultivating the interior life and withdrawing from the world. I don't know about that—nor do I think Mr. Dreher had any real understanding of the specific liturgical foundation (Catholic traditionalism) of this monastery's life. What is clear, however, is that, thanks to the power of Catholic Tradition, a monastery like Norcia can almost immediately assume spiritual leadership—even in the secular world.

These examples illustrate the disproportionate influence of contemplative communities among traditionalists, other Roman Catholics, and even the nonreligious. Primarily, of course, it is their liturgies, prayers, and chant which are transformative. And it seems that, just as in the days of the Benedictine monks of the "Dark Ages," a host of secular benefits seem to flow from this spiritual foundation.

Another development, largely dating from 2013 and afterward, is the readiness of distinguished members of the hierarchy to regularly speak at traditionalist conferences, to preside at ordinations in the traditional form, and to

celebrate traditional liturgies. Bishop Athanasius Schneider
and Cardinal Raymond Burke are the most prominent—
fearless defenders not just of the traditional liturgy but of
Catholic morality. Cardinal Burke and Cardinal Zen have
also spoken on the tragic situation of the Church in China.
We might add to this list the "underground" statements of
Archbishop Viganò on the current state of the Church. It
is an array of public ecclesiastical advocates unimaginable
just ten years ago. Of course, of the above, only Cardinal
Burke is an American—but I could add the names of
several supportive bishops in the United States who have
offered public support to traditionalists.

On the intellectual front, there have been definite gains
in focus and understanding in the last eight years. In this
realm, however, most people make little distinction between
conservatives, traditionalists, and, for that matter, others
not Christian at all (like the French authors M. Onfray
or M. Houellebecq). And isn't one of the best analyses
of the Novus Ordo Mass *Work of Human Hands* by the
late Fr. Anthony Cekada (a sedevacantist)? Adherents of
traditionalism also regularly read the online publications
of the conservative Catholics that I have previously listed.
Specifically traditionalist sites of general interest—com-
bining news, commentary, essays, and politics—that can
be added are *Rorate Caeli* and *OnePeterFive*.

The distinction between American and foreign authors
is also relatively meaningless. It is still a fact that American traditionalism relies heavily on writers from Europe:
Martin Mosebach, Roberto de Mattei, Aldo Maria Valli,
Fr. Michael Fiedrowicz, Fr. Claude Barthe—to name some
of the more prominent. Some of these authors' works have
been translated; much has not. It's still a great advantage
for a traditionalist to be able to understand a number of
foreign languages: French, German, Italian, and Spanish,

both in order to read the above-mentioned authors and also to follow numerous informative online publications in those languages (e.g., *Le Forum Catholique*).

This is not to say that the American and other English-speaking traditionalists have been idle. Let me mention just a few names. Dr. Peter Kwasniewski has become a ubiquitous presence as both a speaker and a writer, primarily analyzing liturgical questions. His four books dedicated to the Latin Mass have been popular, especially the most recent of them, *Reclaiming Our Roman Catholic Birthright* (Angelico Press, 2020). Dr. John Lamont has written on theological, moral, and philosophical issues of the past but also on the deviations of the contemporary Church. Dr. John Rao continues to explore history from a traditionalist perspective as he has been doing for decades now. His Lake Garda conference (which was held on Long Island this year) has served for many years as a forum for traditionalists. It fulfills on the intellectual level much the same role that that the Chartres pilgrimage has done on the liturgical front. Finally, to this group we must of course add the online apostolate of Fr. John Hunwicke of England, as well as the work of Dr. Joseph Shaw of the Latin Mass Society.

Let me give examples of specific topics that have received more careful consideration than had been the case in the past. New objects of inquiry are the Mass texts themselves: the readings, the orations, the Holy Week liturgies. Articles analyzing the Mass texts in detail have appeared on the popular sites *New Liturgical Movement* and *Rorate Caeli*. This research makes impossible, without significant further qualification, the former traditionalist objective, so glibly asserted years ago, of merely restoring the Latin Mass as it was done right before the Council. I should point out that the New Liturgical Movement ("NLM") is now a venue where real knowledge is thoughtfully presented.

In a similar vein, in the fields of theology and history, I might mention the growing realization that all was not well prior to 1958, that the foundations for the explosion of the Second Vatican Council were laid well before 1962. Indeed, the entire era characterized by nineteenth-century ultramontanism (1846–1958) now appears, seen in perspective, in large part a preparation for the collapse of the 1960s. Some analyses of the roots of the Council go back much further than that. Once again, it is no longer possible, without significant qualifications, to contrast the postconciliar chaos with a preconciliar Eden.

A third, more abstruse, even exotic, topic is integralism. I have classified this movement in Part 1 of this essay as "conservative Catholic," given its "papalist" orientation. From another point of view, however, integralism intersects with traditionalism. For example, in advocating the subordination of the temporal to the spiritual power it directly clashes with the direction taken by the Second Vatican Council as well as with the neoconservative ideology of the "American experiment." Now and then one is even reminded of *Triumph* magazine! *The Josias*, the movement's website, features contributions by a number of traditionalist "greats" covering a wide range of topics from the integralist perspective.

The foregoing presentation is of necessity incomplete. I hope I will not have offended anyone left out! To form a complete list today of all monastic communities, Catholic intellectuals, and websites would be a task greatly exceeding the scope of a short essay like this. My intent is, by giving representative examples known to me, to demonstrate that traditionalism in America has progressed far beyond the stage of being content with just celebrating the Old Mass for a circle of initiates. It has become a broader force for general Catholic reform.

IV

BY EARLY SUMMER OF 2021, CATHOLIC TRADI-
tionalists had emerged from the grip of the coronavirus
panic. They had survived in better shape than anyone
perhaps expected. Throughout the crisis, traditionalist
priests *on the whole* had maintained a more generous
schedule of Masses and had interpreted the restrictions
much more liberally than elsewhere in the Church. This
was not just because of conservative political suspicion of
the whole affair. Rather, it reflected the foundational traditionalist principle that preserving the Mass and the whole
of Catholic tradition for the Christian people overrides
"following the rules"—both ecclesiastical and secular—that
is otherwise the governing axiom of the Catholic Church.

We continue to witness the beneficial consequences of
Summorum Pontificum. The multitude of lists of Masses
reported on this site [the Society of St. Hugh of Cluny]—
and their photographic record—speaks for itself. Just in
one corner of my own diocese some five traditionalist
priests are now active where none were found five years
ago. Remarkable, above all, is the outward, evangelical
focus of traditionalism today. Young priests, both secular
and religious, celebrate the traditional Mass without regard
to the consequences to their own careers. The laity—as
always, the dominant supporters of the celebration of the
Old Mass—publicize Masses, processions, and devotions
by word and image. Now, in some corners, the old fears
of publicity and of confrontation with clerical authority
remain—I am thinking especially of the *Ecclesia Dei* communities. But this is now a receding aspect of traditionalist life!

American traditionalism retains its spontaneous, voluntary, even undisciplined character. I certainly admire the
ties that exist in France between Catholic traditionalism
and patriotic, monarchist, and even Maurrassian currents.

This is not a defect, but a strength—no wonder traditionalism first coalesced as a major movement in France! In the United States, however, virtually no "infrastructure" of this kind exists; no favorable social or cultural milieu supports preserving the Old Mass. And traditionalism offers no economic or career benefits. As noted above, there is a perception that a cleric or seminarian who espouses traditionalism has thereby given up any hopes of ecclesiastical preferment. In the United States, people commit to the traditional Mass because they want to—regardless of the consequences. And, as ever, traditionalism wins its new adherents only one by one—by offering to individuals the opportunity of experiencing the traditional liturgy. Traditionalism continues on its chosen path regardless of whether millions or a handful join its ranks.

I would further note the increasing resilience traditionalists display today. Inevitably, their rise generates conflicts with the clerical establishment (more on that later!). And even where no "ideological" confrontation exists, just the embedding, in accordance with the principles of *Summorum Pontificum*, of traditionalist communities within the established Church exposes them to all the ills of twenty-first-century Catholicism. I am familiar, for example, with a parish described some fifteen years ago as a *"Molokai"* for clerical "troublemakers"—originally none of them traditionalists! This church gradually adopted the celebration of the traditional Mass as its guiding—not exclusive—liturgical feature. That attracted new parishioners, families, and apostolates (musical, liturgical, artistic and educational—even a lavish coffee hour!). What had been an elderly church teetering on the brink of collapse had become a center of Catholic life—dare I even use that Catholic cliché, "vibrant"? Within the last few years and for a variety of reasons, however, the original leadership was scattered—two priests now reside outside the diocese, one is deceased, one has been retired, and one has been assigned the duties of chaplain to a nursing home. Yet the celebration of the traditional Mass at this parish continues—after the coronavirus, once more with exemplary music and ceremony. Moreover, former parishioners of that parish—also scattered—have helped to found or expand some half dozen traditional Mass communities. The same observation can be made of the young priests who are often reassigned to the fringes of their dioceses: they then use the opportunity to build up the traditionalist ministry there. Traditionalists cannot escape the problems of the Church—yet every reverse they suffer seems to yield an even greater harvest!

The Unfolding Attack against Traditionalism

Of course, I could not foresee when I started this series of posts just a month ago that a long-feared Vatican move against traditionalists would begin to take concrete form and indeed may be imminent. As always, I would recommend waiting to see what—if anything—emerges. People forget, for example, that in 2011, according to well-founded rumors, a move was underfoot in the Vatican to undercut *Summorum Pontificum* by issuing restrictive regulations on its implementation. When, however, the actual guidelines emerged (in an Instruction entitled *Universae Ecclesiae*), *Summorum Pontificum* had only been reconfirmed. So let us see what actually is published. Moreover, some of the rumored restrictions (such as requiring diocesan priests to obtain permission from their bishop to celebrate the traditional Mass) resemble how *Summorum Pontificum* is in fact administered today in most places—as a variant of the *Ecclesia Dei* indult.

The key consequence, however, will be a change in the political atmosphere. Any such document issued by the pope, whatever its operative provisions, will confirm once more the status of traditionalists as an alien *enemy within* of the Catholic Church. It will send a clear message to bishops and religious orders that they now can take any restrictive actions against traditionalists they deem appropriate without fearing any correction from Rome. Every clerical careerist will understand that protecting traditionalists will be detrimental to his further rise in the organization.

Already we see evidence of such effects—what the Germans call "preemptive obedience." In France, a long-established FSSP apostolate in Dijon was summarily terminated without explanation or discussion with any of the affected parties. Here in Connecticut a traditional Mass in the local Cathedral has been terminated without any reason being given. I would expect such examples to multiply.

The Ideological Basis of a Crisis

Traditionalists should not be surprised. For at the root of it all is a profoundly ideological disagreement with the "Second Vatican Council"—by which I mean the totality of changes introduced between 1962 and 1970. I would best summarize these developments as a process of conformity to the world of modernity. The leadership of the Catholic Church expected thereby to bridge over the gulf that existed between the modern world and the Church, to dissolve an alleged Catholic ghetto.

From its very inception, Vatican II failed in its mission of securing a safe home for Catholicism in modernity. On basic issues touching in one way or another every human family—divorce, birth control, abortion, homosexuality, euthanasia—modernity continually offered new developments ever more irreconcilable with the principles of Christianity—and even with those of rationality itself. In turn, the Catholic Church came to resemble more and more one of the many monotonous bureaucracies of secular modernity: a business corporation, a government ministry, or an educational institution. Given the institutional Church's growing resemblance in style and substance to the secular establishment, certainly in the developed world, the laity, clergy, and religious saw no further need to remain in it. The result of Vatican II was an institutionalized, unresolvable crisis for the Church: declining Catholic resources coupled with unremitting pressure from the secular world, exercised in a hundred ways, for further conformity to its agenda.

Traditionalists are those who acknowledge no obligation to conform to modernity, who dispute the modern world's claim to embody a final revelation. They emphatically deny to the modern age any semi-divine nature—indeed, for them "the world" has negative or ambiguous associations. Following the words of their Founder, Catholic traditionalists understand conflict with this world to be a normal aspect of life for the Church—not a regrettable tragedy. The concrete expression of these principles is the celebration of the traditional Mass—a form of worship that arose entirely outside of the culture, politics, and ideology of modernity.

Accordingly, regardless of what they might be saying about these broad spiritual topics, just by celebrating the old Mass traditionalists constitute a reproach to the ideology of the establishment in a way, let us say, that pro-abortion Catholics do not. The indictment is all the stronger in that the traditionalists are growing, not declining. Their flourishing holds up an unflattering mirror to the failure of the grand dreams of the Council. From the beginning hostility was inevitable, since the institutional Church, like its secular equivalents, is incapable of self-reflection or of reexamining its principles. No "hermeneutic of reform in continuity" could resolve this "clash of cultures."

Actions such as those Pope Francis is contemplating are proof of the establishment's weakness, not its strength. The need to stoop to strong-arm tactics only demonstrates how little authority Vatican II actually has. We might say the same about Bishop Barron's claim that the documents of the Council need to be better explained. But hasn't the Church been doing that for 60 years? Are we not admitting that the verbose documents of the Council are themselves the greatest barrier to understanding?

Nor do I think the political context is right for this kind of thing. Any measures taken against traditionalists will be juxtaposed with the ongoing synodal path in Germany—which Francis himself is fostering. Nor will comparisons be lacking with Francis's efforts to derail consideration of the abortion issue in the Church in the United States. Potential restrictive measures against traditionalists of course constitute a clear change of course from *Summorum Pontificum*, issued just fourteen years ago—a sense of bad faith on the part of the hierarchy is all too perceptible. Observers will also be struck by the contrast between the Pope's treatment of a more youthful, growing segment of the Church and the favor shown to groups in decline: the mainstream religious orders, much of the educational system, the European episcopates, etc. The consequence of these reflections will be a further massive loss of credibility for the Catholic Church.

Do I need to add that these rumored actions are an incredible insult to the author of *Summorum Pontificum*, Pope Benedict, who, after all, is still alive? That they are further evidence of how correct was the course of the FSSPX in rejecting various offers of reconciliation by the Vatican—the last such formal occasion being in 2012?

"Stay the Course!"

Given the above facts, I would advise calm. Tradition-alism is strong. Traditionalists should continue as before and let their opponents make the first moves. Certainly our Society of St. Hugh of Cluny is developing several major projects for the second half of this year—and we are assuming that they will be realized. Sharing of information among traditionalists will be, however, critical. Over the years, we have often remarked on the lamentable commu-nication gaps that exist right here in the New York area, let alone nationwide. Fortunately, attempts to address this deficiency are already underway.

What if significant restrictions are imposed? Could the experience of adversity even be beneficial to American traditionalism? The French website *Paix Liturgique*, in an important essay, reviewed the French experience leading up to the indults and *Summorum Pontificum*. It high-lighted an important fact—often overlooked by American traditionalists—that the gradual recovery of the right to the traditional Mass was not a disinterested gift of the Vatican, of Popes John Paul II and Benedict. Rather it was a right fought for and won by the efforts of many among the clergy and laity—principally, of course, Arch-bishop Lefebvre and his followers. Starting as early as the 1960s, their activity created public pressure that eventually induced the Vatican to progressively lift restrictions on the traditional Mass.

The American experience was different. Here, prior to the indults, the work of the FSSPX and of the indepen-dent priests was more marginal. The permission for the traditional Mass in the 1980s was, from the American perspective, a gratefully received gift from above. Will Americans fight to defend these rights, apparently so easily obtained?

I am confident that the answer to that question is yes. For since the 1980s traditionalists here have had more experience of working together. Moreover, they have on occasion stood their ground against authority when challenged. For example, when in 2014 the New York Archdiocese proposed closing Holy Innocents church—one of three Manhattan parishes that regularly celebrated the traditional Mass—parishioners organized a massive action involving extensive publicity in secular media. And the key argument of the defense was preserving the traditional Mass in New York—its celebration at Holy Innocents was illustrated by a beautiful video. Ultimately the archdiocese backed down and to the present day Holy Innocents remains an active parish with an ever-growing congregation. Not all actions challenging the targeted closing of traditionalist parishes have been as successful. But traditionalists can learn from these campaigns—if the need presents itself.

The only real danger I see is that traditionalists would succumb to the temptation to conform to the establishment, to water down the message of traditionalism in order to reach an accommodation with the ruling ecclesiastical powers. We have experienced in the not-too-distant past traditionalists engaging in self-censorship in an attempt to win the favor of the clerical masters of this or that parish, diocese, or order. And at the present moment, we see the related phenomenon on the internet of alleged traditionalists such as Steve Skojec and Michael Warren Davis launching attacks against traditionalists—employing rhetoric similar to that employed by Pope Francis, Bishop Barron, the French episcopate, etc.

Such tactics, assuming they are meant honestly in the first place, are extremely shortsighted. Do these people imagine that the "powers that be" of the Church will for one moment agree to any kind of durable compromise on such matters? Their actions and statements are only welcome to them as a tool for discrediting traditionalists.

For the strength of traditionalism is its nature as a spiritual and religious movement—in contrast to the ideology of today's Catholic establishment. Beyond all discussions of tactics, traditionalism's aim always remains the greater glory of God, not arranging an accommodation with worldly powers or achieving secular economic or social goals. Catholic traditionalism will remain vital as long as it adheres to these principles, however "rigid" and "unyielding" they may be.

Up to the present-day, traditionalists have kept this faith. And some sixty years of experience have shown that people will continue to respond to this message. *"Never ask if meaning it, wanting it, warned of it—men go"* (Gerard Manly Hopkins). The saga of American Catholic traditionalism will undoubtedly offer many more surprising and glorious chapters!

10 *Traditionis Custodes*

DISPATCHES FROM
THE FRONT

ON JULY 16, POPE FRANCIS STARTED A war. Regardless of the specific provisions of his motu proprio, all Catholic traditionalists, as such, have been declared enemies of the Church. They are deprived of all liturgical rights and are to be segregated from the body of Catholics. The bishops of the Catholic Church are, in practice, empowered to tolerate or absolutely prohibit the traditional Mass—at their arbitrary discretion. The ultimate objective is the total disappearance of the traditionalists. At the Vatican further measures accompanying *Traditionis Custodes* ("TC"—by this term I also include the Pope's cover letter) are reported to be in the course of preparation: restrictions to be imposed on the *Ecclesia Dei* orders, and even more restrictive regulations implementing TC.

It is a war not just against "groups" (the contemptuous terminology of TC) but against families, young children, diocesan and religious priests, seminarians, established parishes, and dedicated congregations. It is a struggle against a movement that is spread, to a greater or lesser extent, over the entire world. This conflict will also be played out in religious communities, schools, and individual families. It will even spill over into the "conservative" Novus Ordo realm, given the close ties of every kind that exist between the adherents of that tendency in the Church and the traditionalists.[1]

Everywhere there is a sense that a boundary has been crossed, that the Church has moved into new and uncharted waters. War does have the advantage of clarifying issues and power relationships, of advancing from mystification to reality. However, the "fortunes of war" are inherently unpredictable. A nation, like France in 1870, may enter into war, as its prime minister at that time, Émile Ollivier, said, "with a light heart." So did all Europe in 1914, Germany in Russia in 1941, Japan at Pearl Harbor later that same year, and the United States subsequently in Vietnam, Iraq, and Afghanistan. In all these cases, the confrontation that emerged was unimaginably different from the assumptions governing at the beginning. The Roman Catholic Church will shortly be experiencing the same.

Moreover, Pope Francis has declared his intent to conduct that most difficult of martial undertakings, an aggressive war of annihilation. As Martin van Creveld once pointed out, such a war, by leaving the enemy only two outcomes—victory or extinction—dramatically solidifies the enemy's will to resist regardless of what his previous political or military weakness may have been.[2] In this respect, TC is the "Operation Barbarossa" of the Church.

So far, the traditionalists have stood fast. With a few exceptions, the laity have not yielded to anger, panic, or despair. Nor have they surrendered to the establishment, even though confronted by a hostile papal will. Quite rightly, they have "stayed the course," letting the hierarchy take the first steps. Public prayers and recitations of the

---

1 For an analysis, see Peter Kwasniewski, "Why Restricting the TLM Harms Every Parish Mass," *Crisis Magazine*, August 13, 2021.
2 *The Transformation of War* (New York: Free Press, 1991), 142–45.

rosary have multiplied. According to my observations—as well as those of several other informed observers—attendance at local traditional Masses has actually increased. And this jump in attendance in the "off-season" of Summer is not just due to the revived piety of the traditionalist communities! For one consequence of TC and the resulting uproar is that, among those Catholics who actually practice their faith, many more people have now heard of "traditionalism" and wish to experience what all the fuss is about. From what I know, the clergy who celebrate the Old Mass—in the New York area, overwhelmingly diocesan priests—have also calmly, collectively, and with dignity defended their adherence to Catholic Tradition.

The hierarchy are the designated enforcers of TC. So far, the bishops fall roughly into two camps. In those dioceses where there is a significant traditionalist presence the policy so far generally has been to preserve the status quo. Perhaps this is because such bishops have had the opportunity over the years of working with traditionalists and thus cannot share the indictment set forth in TC. More cynically, these bishops realize that they would be the real point men of Pope Francis's war and foresee the adverse personnel, finance, and media consequences that an all-out attack on a substantial Catholic community might entail. For example, in one diocese in the New York area with which I am familiar, more than 10% of the diocesan priests celebrate the traditional Mass. If we counted only active priests, that percentage would be greater. I should add that in some prominent dioceses neither the bishop nor the Catholic media has made any mention of TC at all up till now—testimony to its explosive nature. However, it is also true that major and minor incidents of harassment have occurred in certain of the "status quo" dioceses, like the cancellation of a Pontifical Mass in Washington, DC.

In the other camp are those dioceses where traditionalist Catholics are few or where the bishop is more fanatically ideological. Here drastic restrictions or even prohibitions on the traditional Mass have been immediately and summarily imposed. Fortunately for most Americans, such dioceses are more frequently found outside the United States and especially in the Latin world. Some of the harshest anti-traditionalist measures, moreover, have been taken in regions, such as the Czech Republic or Central America, where the Catholic Faith is in complete collapse. Is it not strange? For a Catholic bishop to prohibit Masses, expel religious orders, prevent pilgrimages, and shut down parishes—as did the communists and anticlericals of yore—is now a badge of loyalty to the Pope!

I have been heartened by the amazing outpouring of commentary on TC—mostly sympathetic to traditionalism and from a broad spectrum of Catholics (and non-Catholics). It is hard to single out individual contributions in such a bountiful harvest. But are we really surprised that one of the earliest and at the same time most "theological" analyses came from the hand of Michel Onfray, a French atheist? If someone had told me in 2005 that the quintessential "conservatives" Amy Welborn and George Weigel one day would be writing in defense of traditionalists I would have considered him mad—yet both now have given us perceptive contributions. In the context of their names I might also cite Rod Dreher (now Eastern Orthodox). The experienced advocates of the Old Rite or at least of Catholic Tradition have of course been outspoken. I might mention, among many others, Cardinals Burke, Zen, and Sarah, Martin Mosebach, Fr. John Hunwicke, Bishop Athanasius Schneider, and Peter Kwasniewski. Even certain major progressive Catholic media outlets such as *katholisch.de*, the house organ of the ultraliberal German

Catholic Church, have been decidedly ambivalent on TC, with articles criticizing the motu proprio appearing in these forums. Perhaps one reason for their reserve (and that of certain progressive clerics) is that TC took most of them completely by surprise too.

The pro-traditionalist reaction has not been confined to the Catholic media: articles defending traditionalism have appeared on the pages of the *Wall Street Journal* and the *New York Times*! Cardinal Sarah's powerful essay appeared in *Le Figaro* in France and Michel Onfray's in *Figaro.fr*. I look forward to a publication of an anthology of these contributions, each of which illuminates the issue from a different perspective and the whole representing a veritable encyclopedia of traditionalist belief. It will be an invaluable reference for Catholic traditionalists—or for the curious outsider who wants to discover what motivates these people.[3]

We ask ourselves: what has prompted TC? I do not believe for a minute that it was occasioned by the traditionalists' "rejection" either of Vatican II or of the validity of the Novus Ordo. In most traditionalist communities and events I hear little or nothing on these subjects. Rather, 99.99% of the recent criticism of the Church has related not to Vatican II, but to the actions and initiatives of Pope Francis over the last eight years: his management of the Vatican with its unending series of scandals, *Amoris Laetitia*, his treatment of the Church in China, the "Amazonian" synod and Pachamama, the mishandling of the ongoing sexual abuse crisis, the pope's ambiguous response to the Synodal Path in Germany, his intervention in the abortion

---

3 This anthology, containing 70 responses written by cardinals, bishops, priests, religious, and laity, was published in 2021 by Angelico Press under the title *From Benedict's Peace to Francis's War: Catholics Respond to the* Motu Proprio Traditionis Custodes *on the Latin Mass.*

debate in the United States—to list only some of the
"highlights" of his papacy. The overall tendency can be
summarized as a return to progressive radicalism in theology, morality, and politics—to an understanding of Vatican
II and its liturgy as a clean break with the Church's past.

Opponents of all these developments soon made themselves heard. Traditionalists represented only a minority of
these critics. But it is true that, consciously or not, those
who object to one or all of these policies start to gravitate
to the traditionalist movement—even if they do not at
first become committed traditionalists. This is because
traditionalism represents not only liturgical but also moral
and theological continuity with the Church of all time. As
a result of these controversies, initiated by Pope Francis,
traditionalism paradoxically received a new impetus.

But the expansion of traditionalism is not just because
of conflicts over fundamental issues at the highest level of
the Church. A growing number of families found traditionalism the best practical way to live the faith, to raise their
children as Christians, and to experience stability, beauty,
and community in the Church. The same can be said of
the growing number of young priests who celebrate the Old
Mass, for they have discovered in Catholic Tradition a fuller
priestly life. These younger clergy are found not only in the
Ecclesia Dei orders and traditionalist monasteries—which,
at least in the United States, have to turn away aspiring
seminarians for lack of space. They include graduates of the
diocesan seminaries and members of the "establishment"
religious orders, who have discovered traditionalism—often
in the face of bitter hostility from their superiors and bishops. In most cases, these priests have had no objections
in principle to celebrating the Novus Ordo when that is
appropriate. In the case of this younger rising generation of
priests and laity, moreover, Catholic traditionalism has not

been a legacy from the past, but an entirely spontaneous and freely chosen expression of the Faith.

This vitality contrasts with the irreversible decline of the official Church and its institutions. Only 20–30% of Catholics regularly practice the faith in the United States—and these statistics are excellent compared to Germany or France. In more recent years "non-practicing Catholics" turn more and more frequently into outright nonbelievers. In addition, in the United States, and to much greater extent in most of Latin America, there is steady hemorrhaging to fundamentalist Protestantism. The establishment has discovered no answer to the crisis of vocations. Nor has it been able to put its finances on a sound footing or end the relentless pressure of lawyers and prosecutors on the sex abuse front.

The contrast, at least in the developed world, between the progress of the traditionalist movement—despite its limited absolute numbers—and the ineffectiveness of the official Church was growing ever greater. For just the very existence of the traditionalists is eloquent commentary on the failures of the institutional Church. The youth and spontaneity of the traditionalists contrasted more and more strongly with the centralization, bureaucracy, and ever-growing average age of the clergy, religious, and laity in most of the establishment Church. And the celebration of the Old Mass was spreading from the nations where it had been "traditionally" strong (like the United States) into new territory (like Italy). Moreover, as we have seen, traditionalism serves as a focus for those deeply disturbed by the dire non-liturgical problems in the Church. For all these reasons, the leadership of the Catholic Church, instead of addressing the causes of its underlying problems, has now launched a campaign with the ultimate aim of eliminating the traditionalist movement entirely.

Now the Church does not exist in a vacuum but always is situated in a concrete historical context. It is, after all, no coincidence that Vatican II took place in the same decade as did the student revolts (of 1968 in Europe, earlier in the United States) and even the Chinese "Cultural Revolution." These were all movements of massive change emanating not from the grassroots or the revolutionary masses but instigated and led by institutional leadership or a privileged elite. Similarly, the secular background of TC is the rising totalitarian tide in the United States and Western Europe evident, at the latest, since the 2016 United States presidential elections. It involves the consolidation of all the institutions of Western civil society (government, law, education, business, etc.) into a unified bloc with a defined ideology (ecology, anti-COVID, movements of social revolution summarized as "woke"). Enemies, dissenters, or those who simply remain silent are demonized in the media, censored, subjected to punitive consequences regarding their business or employment, compelled to confess their "guilt" or undergo reeducation and, in some situations, physically threatened. Even more so than in the 1960s, it is a "revolution from above" of the rich and the powerful.

These tendencies of course influence the Vatican, especially given its eagerness to please the secular media and economic powers of the West. Indeed, the Vatican has been in direct contact with the secular leaders of some of these specific initiatives, which the Church has endorsed or at least benevolently tolerated. So in a sense TC can be seen as the transposition into the Catholic Church of the West's current "totalitarian moment," sharing its insistence on external unity as an absolute value and its demand for unquestioning adherence to the ruling establishment. Some of the confrontational rhetoric of the letter accompanying TC and of the motu proprio's defenders is even identical to that of the secular establishment: the need to combat with punitive measures "divisive," "ideological," "aggressive" extremists who "endanger unity" and "expose (the Church) to the peril of division."

In a sense, TC should encourage traditionalists, for the Pope has singled out them and the traditional Mass as the one true alternative to the current regime and its ideology. This time of purgation may also be helpful for us, because despite its successes, all was not well in the movement. The real problems were not the anti-institutional zealots active on the internet or elsewhere. On the contrary, the real difficulties resulted from the ever-greater integration of the traditionalists into the structures of the establishment with all its associated defects. Traditionalism, for example, has not at all been immune from instances of clerical sexual abuse. The celebration of the Old Mass, if it occurred in a parish, remained very much contingent on the attitude of the pastor—a change in leadership often brought drastic consequences for the community given the different theological "universes" that the clergy often inhabit today.

Certain traditionalist orders and organizations gradually slipped into a fantasy world regarding the benevolence of the institutional Church, their influence on it, and their insight into its doings. Others, imitating the practices of groups like Opus Dei, tried to resurrect the pristine, intact, preconciliar world by a highly selective reading of Vatican actions and documents (e.g., by emphasizing Pope Francis's 2021 "Year of St. Joseph"). Then, there were those who tried to tone down traditionalism, to censor sermons and conference speakers, and to control public perceptions of reality—all in the fond hope of obtaining the favor of bishops and mainstream religious orders. I don't know about traditionalists' alleged hostility to "the Council," but I can certainly testify to the animosity that could crop up in dealings among the traditionalists and pseudo-traditionalists themselves in the two years prior to TC. I would hope that the new hot war can at least alleviate these grudges and make the traditionalists refocus on their foundational principles. For we will all now be forced to work together for the sake of a cause much greater than ourselves and will need to put aside the petty grievances of the past.

I'll conclude these reflections with one more historical thought. William Lind has observed that just when the established order deems everything to be fixed, settled, and secure and the future looks predictable, history goes off in a wildly different direction. So it was in Europe in August 1914. We see the same phenomenon unfolding in Kabul in these very days. Lind, drawing on an obscure book by William Gerhardie, a less well-known British novelist of the 1930s, calls this *God's Fifth Column*. His message is that the structures of Church and State that we assume to be so solid as to stand forever can collapse with amazing speed.[4]

We do not know what the future may bring for the Church and for traditionalism. And neither does the Vatican. What we do know are the very great graces we and our families have received by adhering to the fullness of Catholic Tradition. We also know that Someone else is at work whose active will is usually left out of our calculations. Therefore I would recommend prayer and patience and trust that God, who does not lead anyone who trusts in Him astray, will take care of things in ways now unforeseeable by us.

---

4   William Lind, "God's Fifth Column," *The American Conservative*, July 17, 2021. Of course, in hindsight, everyone claims the eventual historical outcome to be obvious!

Appendix I

HISTORICAL DOCUMENTS

Exhibit A

DIOCESE OF FRESNO
CHANCERY OFFICE
1890 NORTH FRESNO STREET •
FRESNO, CALIFORNIA
TELEPHONE (AREA CODE 209) 237-0129

MAILING ADDRESS
POST OFFICE BOX 1668
FRESNO, CALIFORNIA 93717

February 13, 1976

Dear Monsignor/Father:

It has come to my attention that the Tridentine Mass has been more common in the Diocese of Fresno than I had reason to suspect .

I wish you to make it a matter of conscience to discover if such a Mass is being celebrated in any hall, house or wherever within the confines of your parish

If so, I wish you to definitely confront the priest if possible and tell him he has no faculties or permission in this Diocese to offer any Mass. If any of his followers are present tell them that the Mass is gravely illicit and that they are gravely sinning through destroying the unity of Faith by their disobedience.

If such a practice continues I will be forced to use the ultimate decision of declaring them contumacious and excommunicated

Sincerely in Christ,

HUGH A DONOHOE
Bishop of Fresno
HAD:g

CL 76: 8

It has been suggested by the USCC:
The following petition is suggested for insertion into the general intercessions on March 14 in the parishes of your diocese:

That there be an alleviation of the suffering experienced by the Jews living in Syria and that they may be free to move and to emigrate as they desire, let us pray to the Lord.

109

DIOCESE OF FRESNO

CHANCERY OFFICE
[Address and phone number]

February 13, 1976

Dear Monsignor/Father:

It has come to my attention that the Tridentine Mass has been more common in the Diocese of Fresno than I had reason to suspect.

I wish you to make it a matter of conscience to discover if such a Mass is being celebrated in any hall, house or wherever within the confines of your parish.

If so, I wish you to definitely confront the priest if possible and tell him he has no faculties or permission in this Diocese to offer any Mass. If any of his followers are present tell them that the Mass is gravely illicit and that they are gravely sinning through destroying the unity of Faith by their disobedience.

If such a practice continues I will be forced to use the ultimate decision of declaring them contumacious and excommunicated.

Sincerely in Christ,
(signature)
HUGH A. DONOHOE
Bishop of Fresno
HAD:g

Cl 76: 8

It has been suggested by the USCC:
The following petition is suggested for insertion into the general intercessions on March 14 in the parishes of your diocese:

> That there be an alleviation of the suffering experienced by the Jews living in Syria and that they may be free to move and to emigrate as they desire, let us pray to the Lord.

Exhibit B

REMBERTUS GEORGIUS

Miseratione Divina et Apostolicae Sedis Gratia

Archiepiscopus Milvauchiensis

February 19, 1985

Milwaukee, Wisconsin

Dear

      The Sacred Congregation for Divine Worship at the Vatican announced in a letter to all diocesan bishops on October 3, 1984 that they could grant a faculty for the limited use of the Tridentine Mass in their diocese. The Congregation's letter also stated that for this permission a petition would need to be submitted to the diocesan bishop by those persons interested in participation in a Tridentine Mass and that certain conditions would need to be satisfied.

      The petition that was submitted by you satisfies the papal conditions and therefore,

      THE ARCHBISHOP OF MILWAUKEE GRANTS YOU PERMISSION TO ATTEND THE ECCLESIASTICALLY APPROVED TRIDENTINE MASS THAT WILL BE CELEBRATED WITHIN THE ARCHDIOCESE OF MILWAUKEE IN THE FUTURE.

- -

Special Notes:

   1) In order to be admitted to the Tridentine Mass you will need to submit this letter of permission at the entrance of the chapel where the Mass is celebrated.

   2) This permission is granted to you and is <u>not</u> able to be extended to other friends or family members.

   3) The Mass will be celebrated in the Tridentine Rite as found in the <u>1962 Revised Typical Edition of the Roman Missal</u>.

   4) The first ecclesiastically approved Tridentine Mass will be a Low Mass celebrated at St. Joseph Convent Chapel at 1501 South Layton Blvd. in Milwaukee on Saturday, February 23rd, at 7:00 p.m. (Parking will be available behind the chapel, enter off of 29th and Greenfield Ave.)

   5) Attendance at this Mass will satisfy the Sunday Mass obligation for the First Sunday of Lent.

Sincerely yours in Christ,

Vice Chancellor

REMBERTUS GEORGIUS
Miseratione Divina et Apostolicae Sedis Gratia
Archiepiscopus Milvauchiensis

February 19, 1985

Milwaukee, Wisconsin

Dear

        The Sacred Congregation for Divine Worship at the
Vatican announced in a letter to all diocesan bishops on October 3, 1984 that they could grant a faculty for the limited use of
the Tridentine Mass in their diocese. The Congregation's letter
also stated that for this permission a petition would need to be
submitted to the diocesan bishop by those persons interested
in participation in a Tridentine Mass and that certain conditions
would need to be satisfied.

        The petition that was submitted by you satisfies the
papal conditions and therefore,

        THE ARCHBISHOP OF MILWAUKEE GRANTS YOU PER-
        MISSION TO ATTEND THE ECCLESIASTICALLY APPROVED
        TRIDENTINE MASS THAT WILL BE CELEBRATED WITHIN THE
        ARCHDIOCESE OF MILWAUKEE IN THE FUTURE.

- -

Special Notes:

1. In order to be admitted to the Tridentine Mass you will need to
    submit this letter of permission at the entrance of the chapel
    where the Mass is celebrated.

2. This permission is granted to you and is not able to be extended
    to other friends or family members.

3. The Mass will be celebrated in the Tridentine Rite as found in
    the 1962 Revised Typical Edition of the Roman Missal.

4. The first ecclesiastically approved Tridentine Mass will be a
    Low Mass celebrated at St. Joseph Convent Chapel at 1501
    South Layton Blvd. in Milwaukee on Saturday, February 23rd,
    at 7:00 p.m. (Parking will be available behind the chapel, enter
    off of 29th and Greenfield Ave.)

5. Attendance at this Mass will satisfy the Sunday Mass obligation
    for the First Sunday of Lent.

                              Sincerely yours in Christ,
                              (undecipherable)
                              Vice Chancellor

"Posted on a Twitter account called Cream City Catholic, we have here a 1985 letter from the Archdiocese of Milwaukee granting someone permission to attend the traditional Latin Mass. It would be interesting to know what the specific conditions were that had to be satisfied before such permission was granted, as stated in the opening paragraph. We should also note the conditions attached, that the letter had to be presented at the chapel to gain admission, and that the permission could not be extended to anyone else ('not able to be extended to other friends or family members'). If the current news about events in the Church gets you down, remember that only 34 years ago, during the Papacy of a canonized Saint, it was an official part of ecclesiastical law that a bishop could treat the members of his flock in this fashion. Let us remember to thank God for the great gift which he gave to the Church by putting an end to this injustice. 'What earlier generations held as sacred, remains sacred and great for us too, and it cannot be all of a sudden entirely forbidden or even considered harmful.'"

—Adapted from the post by Gregory DiPippo, *New Liturgical Movement*, March 2, 2019

A lady who was personally involved sent her recollections to Mr. DiPippo:

"In case no one has informed you, these are the details of how this event transpired.

"A Latin Mass was announced by the Archdiocese. Everyone had to write to the Chancery Office and give a convincing argument why they should be allowed to attend this Mass. Yes, we know we do not need permission to go to Mass, so it's just something we did to be obedient. We awaited our entry ticket, a letter granting us permission. I was denied. So was my sister and brother.

We were ages 25, 27, and 30 at the time. My brother's fiancée was also denied. Our letters of denial basically said we did not have any reason to be devoted to the Old Mass, therefore DENIED.

"We came to the Church anyway, as no one needs permission to go to Mass. We were told to wait outside of the church. We inquired as to why we were being denied the right to pray before the Blessed Sacrament. We were told it was because we did not have a permission letter for Mass. This is a huge seminary chapel, by the way. After everyone entered who showed their permission letters, we were all let in just minutes before Mass with no time to pray before it began. A lot of people brought letters of permission that had been given to other people who were unable to attend the Mass—no IDs were checked against the holder of the letter. The place was filled with young people. A beautiful Mass was celebrated as if no time had lapsed since the Novus Ordo had relegated it to the dust bin.

"The Archdiocese continued to have Latin Mass at this one remote location once a month on Saturday nights for some time."

Exhibit C

A form from the same period, which the diocese of Buf-
falo, New York, required those who wished to attend the
traditional Mass to fill out and submit.

1. Please state in the space below your reason for your request that Mass be
    celebrated in Latin according to the Roman Missal of 1962.

2. "There must be unequivocal, even public evidence that the...people petitioning
    have no ties with those who impugn the lawfulness and doctrinal soundness of
    the Roman Missal promulgated in 1970 by Pope Paul VI."

    Do you affirm as lawful and doctrinally sound the Roman Missal promulgated
    by Pope Paul VI in 1970?

3. The Holy Father wishes to be responsive to "priests and faithful" who "had
    remained attached to the so-called Tridentine Rite."

    Are you among those people who "had remained attached to the Tridentine Rite?"

4. "The indult is to be used without prejudice to the liturgical reform that is
    to be observed in the life of each ecclesial community." The participation
    in this Mass should not be an occasion for you to cease worshipping according
    to the revised liturgical norms.

I wish to attend the Mass in the Neumann Chapel of St. John the Baptist Parish on
May 26, 1985 at 2:00 P.M. I accept the various provisions of the indult.

Name _____   _____

1. Please state in the space below your reason for your request
    that Mass be celebrated in Latin according to the Roman
    Missal of 1962.

2. "There must be unequivocal, even public evidence that
    the ... people petitioning have no ties with those who impugn
    the lawfulness and doctrinal soundness of the Roman Missal
    promulgated in 1970 by Pope Paul VI."

Do you affirm as lawful and doctrinally sound the Roman Missal promulgated by Pope Paul VI in 1970?

3. The Holy Father wishes to be responsive to "priests and faithful" who "had remained attached to the so-called Tridentine Rite."

    Are you among those people who "had remained attached to the Tridentine Rite?"

4. "The indult is to be used without prejudice to the liturgical reform that is to be observed in the life of each ecclesial community." The participation in this Mass should not be an occasion for you to cease worshipping according to the revised liturgical norms.

I wish to attend the Mass in the Neumann Chapel of St. John the Baptist Parish on May 26, 1985 at 2:00 P. M. I accept the various provisions of the indult.

Name _____

Exhibit D

 DIOCESE OF AUSTIN

October 24, 1988

TO: Individuals Who Have Requested a Latin Mass

FROM: Bishop John McCarthy

RE: The Scheduling of a Tridentine Mass, Sundays at 12:30 P.M., Chapel,
        St. Joseph's Hall (Brothers' Residence) Located on the Campus of St.
        Edward's University

While Our Holy Father is constantly working for unity in the Church, he is at
the same time conscious of the needs of special groups. Of late, I have
received several letters requesting the scheduling of a Tridentine Mass and I
am happy to oblige within the guidelines laid down by the Vatican.

A copy of the directive is attached, but let me point out the three most
important items that will affect us with this Mass that is being scheduled.

    a. Persons making use of this privilege must indicate in a very clear
        manner that they accept the teachings of the Universal Church as
        manifested in the Second Vatican Council.

    b. Mass is to be offered in a chapel rather than in a parish church.

    c. Mass is to be offered only for those who request it.

I have been able to secure the use of the chapel at Holy Cross Hall on the
campus of St. Edward's University in Austin and Father Leon Boarman, C.S.C. has
generously offered to take this Mass each Sunday.

The celebration of this Mass will begin on the first Sunday of Advent at
12:30 P.M.

If, for some reason, Father Boarman is not able to offer the Mass, the Diocese
will certainly endeavor to provide a substitute, but since 99% of our priests
are always scheduled tightly on Sunday morning for parish Masses, you need to
know from the very beginning that there may be occasions when the Mass will not
be celebrated. I hope that those times will be few and far between.

While I hope that this arrangement is satisfactory to you, I would ask you to
be aware that the vast, vast majority of our people prefer to pray in a
language that they understand, and it is the teaching of the Universal Church,
guided by the Holy Spirit, that they be allowed to do so. Please continue to
pray that Christ's Church will grow evermore united.

THE CATHOLIC CHURCH IN CENTRAL TEXAS

1600 NORTH CONGRESS • POST OFFICE BOX 13327 • AUSTIN, TEXAS 78711-3327 • (512) 476-4888

Diocese of Austin
October 24, 1988

TO: Individuals Who Have Requested a Latin Mass

FROM: Bishop John McCarthy

RE: The Scheduling of a Tridentine Mass, Sundays at 12:30
           P. M., Chapel, St. Joseph's Hall (Brothers' Residence)
           Located on the Campus of St. Edward's University

While Our Holy Father is constantly working for unity in the Church,
he is at the same time conscious of the needs of special groups. Of
late, I have received several letters requesting the scheduling of a
Tridentine Mass and I am happy to oblige within the guidelines laid
down by the Vatican.

A copy of the directive is attached, but let me point out the three
most important items that will affect us with this Mass that is being
scheduled.

  a. Persons making use of this privilege must indicate in a very
     clear manner that they accept the teachings of the Universal
     Church as manifested in the Second Vatican Council.

  b. Mass is to be offered in a chapel rather than in a parish church.

  c. Mass is to be offered only for those who request it.

I have been able to secure the use of the chapel at Holy Cross Hall
on the campus of St. Edward's University in Austin and Father Leon
Boarman, C. S. C. has generously offered to take this Mass each Sunday.

The celebration of this Mass will begin on the first Sunday of Advent
at 12:30 P. M.

If, for some reason, Father Boarman is not able to offer the Mass,
the Diocese will certainly endeavor to provide a substitute, but since
99% of our priests are always scheduled tightly on Sunday morning
for parish Masses, you need to know from the very beginning that
there may be occasions when the Mass will not be celebrated. I hope
that those times will be few and far between.

While I hope that this arrangement is satisfactory to you, I would ask
you to be aware that the vast, vast majority of our people prefer to
pray in a language that they understand, and it is the teaching of the
Universal Church, guided by the Holy Spirit, that they be allowed to
do so. Please continue to pray that Christ's Church will grow evermore united.

[Address and phone number]

"A permission slip from the Diocese of Austin, Texas, from October of 1988. The broader indult had only just been issued, and it is nice to see that the bishop, John McCarthy, wrote that he was 'happy to oblige' requests for the celebration of the traditional Mass. Permission was given for a regular Sunday celebration. He also notes that if the appointed celebrant should be unavailable, the diocese will endeavor to provide a substitute, and while he warns that this might not always be possible, he 'hope(s) that those times will be few and far between.' By the standards of the era, this was actually quite generous; I am sure some of our readers remember indult Masses that were highly restrictive or inconvenient as to both time and location. In the later 1990s, I heard of one Sunday indult Mass that foundered because it was celebrated in a terrible neighborhood at 2:30pm."

—Adapted from the post by Gregory DiPippo, *New Liturgical Movement*, March 8, 2019

Exhibit E

St. Josaphat Church welcomes you to the celebration of the Tridentine Rite Latin Mass. This is the only celebration of the traditional Latin Mass in the Archdiocese of Detroit with the approval and permission of Cardinal Adam Maida.

The Tridentine Mass will be celebrated here at St. Josaphat Church every Sunday throughout the year at 9:30 A.M. The Novus Ordo Mass (New Order Mass) will be celebrated on Feast Days and Holy Days. All other sacramental celebrations outside Sunday Mass will be celebrated according to the Novus Ordo in English.

We encourage your generosity in supporting St. Josaphat Parish for its work in providing for this celebration. For persons who intend to regularly attend this celebration of the Tridentine Mass, you may wish to register in the parish to receive the pastoral care and benefits of a parishioner. Parishioners will also receive envelopes and the usual document to file with income tax returns.

Persons who wish to sing in the choir or to usher may sign up in the rear of the church after Mass.

St. Josaphat Church welcomes you to the celebration of the Tridentine Rite Latin Mass. This is the only celebration of the traditional Latin Mass in the Archdiocese of Detroit with the approval and permission of Cardinal Adam Maida.

The Tridentine Mass will be celebrated here at St. Josaphat Church every Sunday throughout the year at 9:30 A.M. The Novus Ordo Mass (New Order Mass) will be celebrated on Feast Days and Holy Days. All other sacramental celebrations outside Sunday Mass will be celebrated according to the Novus Ordo in English.

We encourage your generosity in supporting St. Josaphat Parish for its work in providing for this celebration. For persons who intend to regularly attend this celebration of the Tridentine Mass, you may wish to register in the parish to receive the pastoral care and benefits of a parishioner. Parishioners will also receive envelopes and the usual document to file with income tax returns.

Persons who wish to sing in the choir or to usher may sign up in the rear of the church after Mass.

An authority on the history of the traditional Mass in Detroit offered the following commentary:

"Tamer perhaps than most, this 'discouragement card' was handed out by chancery officials at the first indult Mass in the Archdiocese of Detroit at St. Josaphat Church on October 3, 2004. Its purpose was the following: 1. To explain that Christmas, New Year's, and other Holy Days would not be made available in the TLM. 2. To remind everyone that the Novus Ordo was the norm. 3. To state, in a backhanded way, that altar servers were paid employees of the Archdiocese (students and a teacher hired from University of Detroit Jesuit High School), and volunteers were not welcome.

"Micromanagement of this Mass by the chancery continued a little over two months, until December, 2004, when St. Josaphat administrator Fr. Mark Borkowski pushed back. The chancery people immediately backed off, and the atmosphere immediately converted to that of a healthy, happy, normal parish."

Exhibit F

A D D E N D U M

Help Needed in Assisi - The Custos of the Sacro Convento in Assisi is interested
in securing help with the exceptionally large number of
pilgrims coming to Assisi as a part of their Holy Year pilgrimage. He appeals to
the U.S. friars for anyone who would like to serve as an English-speaking guide
anytime from now till October. The Custos will pay travel expenses and offer "some
personal compensation." Those interested should contact Fr. Venance

The Bishops' Liturgy Commission - The Bishops' Liturgy Commission has asked us to
call the attention of all to the attached memo.
When an episcopal conference has decreed that the vernacular version of the missal
or any of its parts, such as the Order of the Mass, must be employed in its region,
the celebration of the Mass whether in Latin or in the vernacular is lawful only
according to the rites of the Roman Missal promulgated by authority of Paul VI on
April 3, 1969.

With reference to the norms issued by this Congregation for the sake of the priests
who by reason of old age or infirmity experience serious difficulties in observing
the new Order of the Roman Missal Lectionary, it is clear that the Ordinary may
permit them to use the 1962 editio typica of the Roman Missal, adapted by the
decrees of 1965 and 1967. The text, in its entirety or in part, can be used only
for the celebration of the Mass without a congregation. In no way may Ordinaries
grant the faculty for Masses celebrated with a congregation. Rather, Ordinaries---
local and religious--- should be vigilant so that, with the exception of non-Roman
liturgical rites lawfully recognized by the church and notwithstanding any pretext
of custom, even immemorial custom, the Order of Mass of the new Roman Missal may
be correctly accepted and that its content--- may be understood with greater zeal
and reverence by all the priests and faithful of the Roman Rite.

A D D E N D U M

Help Needed in Assisi – The Custos of the Sacro Convento in Assisi is interested in securing help with the exceptionally large number of pilgrims coming to Assisi as part of their Holy Year pilgrimage. He appeals to the U. S. friars for anyone who would like to serve as an Ebglish-speaking [sic] guide anytime from now till October. The Custos will pay travel expenses and offer "some personal compensation." Those interested should contact Fr. Venance

The Bishops' Liturgy Commission – The Bishops' Liturgy Commission has asked us to call the attention of all to the attached memo. When an episcopal conference has decreed that the vernacular version of the missal or any of its parts, such as the Order of the Mass, must be employed in its region, the celebration of the Mass whether in Latin or in the vernacular is lawful only according to the rites of the Roman Missal promulgated by authority of Paul VI on April 3, 1969.

With reference to the norms issued by this Congregation for the sake of the priests who by reason of old age or infirmity experience serious difficulties in observing the new Order of the Roman Missal Lectionary, it is clear that the Ordinary may permit them to use the 1962 editio typica of the Roman Missal, adapted by the decrees of 1965 and 1967. The text, in its entirety or in part, can be used only for the celebration of the Mass without a congregation. In no way may Ordinaries grant the faculty for Masses celebrated with a congregation. Rather, Ordinaries---local and religious---should be vigilant so that, with the exception of non-Roman liturgical rites lawfully recognized by the church and notwithstanding any pretext of custom, even immemorial custom, the Order of Mass of the new Roman Missal may be correctly accepted and that its content---[sic] may be understood with greater zeal and reverence by all the priests and faithful of the Roman Rite.

This document comes from the archives of Dr. John Pepino. He has only the one page, none of the other attachments, so there would be some guesswork as to its exact circumstances. Internal evidence points to a Holy Year pilgrimage sometime after the *Notification* from the Sacred Congregation for Divine Worship (June 14, 1971) on allowing blind or otherwise crippled priests the privilege of saying the traditional Mass (albeit with the 1965 and 1967 modifications) so long as no one else was there to be infected. The next three Holy Years after 1971 are 1975, 1983, 2000. The last date is unlikely since the document is clearly typed on a type-writer (complete with typo on line 4: "Ebglish" for "English"). So it dates to 1975 or 1983. Only more details on "Fr. Venance" could narrow it down.

Appendix II

UNA VOCE:
NOTES TOWARD A HISTORY

UNA VOCE: THE HISTORY OF THE FOEDERATIO Internationalis Una Voce (Leominster: Gracewing, 2017) is an account of Una Voce, one of the main protagonists in Europe, written by a former president of that organization, Leo Darroch. I find it an invaluable contribution to our knowledge of the survival of traditionalism—yet some major reservations and qualifications are necessary.

To start, this book might be more accurately titled *"Materials for* the History of the Foederatio Internationalis Una Voce." For Darroch's book is in no way a complete history of the Una Voce federation, let alone that of post-Vatican II traditionalism. Rather, it is the story of the center or headquarters of the Una Voce organization, its status reports, and above all its discussions over the years with Vatican representatives. The president of Una Voce (International) freely admits that at times he has very little idea of what is happening in the local chapters, where much of the actual work of the federation in education and publication was being done. Some of these, such as the UK and German chapters, were established early and continued to play a major role throughout the period covered by this book. Others, like the United States organization, flowered early, vanished, and reappeared in different reincarnations.

One would very much like to hear more of the experiences of the main national chapters. The Latin Mass

Society of the UK, for example, was involved in the granting in 1971 of the only real concession to the traditional
Mass made by Rome prior to 1984/88: the "English" indult.
(This book, however, makes clear how extremely limited
this concession was.) There is also mention that in some
chapters a more defiant attitude regarding celebrating the
Old Mass continued to exist "under the radar screen" of
the international headquarters.

The format of this book may also be challenging for
readers other than dedicated historians. For the text consists largely of verbatim reports, interviews, minutes of
meetings and letters, at the expense of a coherent nar-
rative. Questions of substance and procedural intricacies,
fundamental discussions of principle, and bureaucratic
trivia are freely mingled here; critical issues arise and
are then suddenly dropped in mid-stream. On the other
hand, a chief contribution of Darroch's book is indeed
the generous selection of excerpts from the original
documents!

We have spoken of the president of Una Voce. This
book is indeed largely the history of one man, Eric de
Saventhem, the founding president of the International
Federation, who sustained the efforts of the federation's
center with his energy, persistence—and, probably, financial resources. It is to his credit, first, that at least some
central point of contact was retained for the "Uniate"
(basically, "non-Lefebvrian") traditionalists. Second, Una
Voce preserved throughout the decades its advocacy of
the preconciliar Mass and never fell into advocating the
so-called Latin (Novus Ordo) Mass that gained such a
hold on "conservative Catholics" in the US. Third, de
Saventhem left us such memorable and visionary statements of principle as:

> A renaissance will come: asceticism and adora-
> tion as the mainspring of direct total dedication
> to Christ will return. Confraternities of priests,
> vowed to celibacy and to an intense life of prayer
> and meditation will be formed. Religious will
> regroup themselves into houses of "strict obser-
> vance." A new form of "Liturgical Movement"
> will come into being, led by young priests and
> attracting young people, in protest against the
> flat, prosaic, philistine or delirious liturgies which
> will soon overgrow and finally smother even the
> recently revised rites...
>
> It is important that these new priests and
> religious, these new young people with ardent
> hearts, should find—if only in a corner of the
> rambling mansion of the Church—the treasure
> of a true sacred liturgy... (Address to the Una
> Voce United States chapter in June 1970)

How could the aspirations be better articulated—and so
early on!—for a movement that would demand so much
personal sacrifice with so little hope of success over so
many decades?

De Saventhem had, however, far less success as a
would-be ecclesiastical politician. His attempts over the
decades to obtain some kind of concession or deal from
the Roman authorities with whom he was in fairly regular
contact had, by his own admission, absolutely no success
prior to the indults of the 1980s. And, as we can infer from
this book, the concessions of the Indults were entirely due
to the efforts of Archbishop Lefebvre, not those of Una
Voce. Indeed, de Saventhem's bureaucratic maneuvers
and proposed compromises served only to undermine the
credibility of a movement allegedly based on the highest
principles. Inevitably, wishful thinking seems to color de
Saventhem's reports. At times, he grasped for signs of
papal favor (under Paul VI!); on other occasions he talks

of parties in the Vatican more or less sympathetic with the traditionalist cause. One feels thrust back into the era of the Cold War Kremlinologists, who in search of the will-o'-the-wisp of détente, constantly sought to identify alleged "moderate" and "hardline" factions in the Soviet leadership. It was a futile endeavor for Una Voce as well: the rudeness, arrogance, and duplicity of the Vatican and the hierarchy in general is laid out here in great detail. One should read this book to understand the FSSPX's well-founded distrust of the Vatican. There is also abundant evidence of the vacillations of Pope John Paul II.

Archbishop Lefebvre, on the other hand, after a late start even subsequent to the foundation of Una Voce, focused on preserving the celebration of the traditional Mass at all costs and, increasingly, regardless of ecclesiastical permissions. To do that he began by training missionary priests in his own seminary, adding schools, communities of sisters, and affiliates such as traditional Benedictines, Dominicans and Redemptorists—and, finally, in his most dramatic step, bishops. It was a course of action that had been put on the table in the early days of the formation of Una Voce but not adopted (at least not by the federation's headquarters). De Saventhem seems to have been in communication now and then with the Archbishop whose movement, in contrast to the static situation of Una Voce, continued its steady and relentless growth.

Of course, this was not just a case of mistaken tactics on the part of de Saventhem. More fundamental factors were in play, whether or not the main players of that era could or would have been willing to articulate them. De Saventhem remained in practice wedded to an "ultramontane" ecclesiology wherein the liturgy was the creation and property of the papacy. Therefore, the principal focus of

Una Voce's center was "negotiations with" (for most of this period, more accurately "supplication of") the relevant Roman authorities. Archbishop Lefebvre, however, given his background as a missionary, must have sensed the radical loss of faith underlying the developments of the 1960s. While Una Voce—or at least its central leadership—saw saving the Mass as a bureaucratic exercise, Lefebvre understood it as a spiritual problem, a challenge of evangelization requiring the radical refounding and reconstitution of Church institutions. Of course, Archbishop Lefebvre's policy was also superior from the purely secular perspective of negotiation tactics (he was, after all, conducting his own discussions with the Holy See). For while de Saventhem could talk to the Roman prelates only of the personal attachment of some of the faithful to the Old Rite, citing petitions and surveys, Lefebvre commanded a growing institutional following that was causing acute embarrassment to Rome. Something had to be done!

The indult of 1984 and even more so the motu proprio *Ecclesia Dei* of 1988 combined with Archbishop Lefebvre's ordination of bishops in that year changed all this. A large number of Lefebvre's priests and affiliates could not follow him in the latter action. Suddenly, Una Voce acquired substantial institutional and clerical allies. Now there was indeed more to talk about at the Vatican as *Ecclesia Dei* was rolled out! Furthermore, the hostility of the Roman authorities softened somewhat and there was a new dialogue partner—the *Ecclesia Dei* commission. Nevertheless, Una Voce had to contend with the unabated hostility to traditionalism of other ecclesiastics in and outside of the Vatican who would continue to defy implementation of the 1988 Indult.

The most dramatic incident of the post-Indult years occurred, however, under the presidency of Michael Davies, who succeeded de Saventhem in 1995. For it was under his watch in 2000 that the future conservative hero, Cardinal Castrillón Hoyos, launched out of a clear blue sky an underhanded attempt to impose "adaptations" derived from the Novus Ordo on the traditional liturgy. Davies and Una Voce, exhibiting greater firmness than the preceding Una Voce administration had shown, resolutely opposed this move. The initiative, which would have destroyed non-FSSPX traditionalism, was quietly allowed to die. Here Una Voce did indeed show its worth.

There are many other gems and curious facts scattered about the pages of this book. It is admittedly incomplete. Yet, if you want to get a sense of what in particular early Catholic traditionalism was like—and the forces it had to contend with—it is a great place to start.

Appendix III

A VIEW FROM OUTSIDE

WAS FASCINATED TO READ A REPORT IN *PAIX Liturgique* on the "epic" of traditionalism in the United States. And not just because of the complimentary reference therein to my own series on the history of Catholic traditionalism! It is always useful to get an outsider's view of one's own world—even though one may not agree with all his conclusions. The French believe, for example, that *The Trouble with Harry* is Alfred Hitchcock's greatest film. It is not, but by understanding their logic one learns a lot about Hitchcock and his movies. On the other hand, Michel Houellebecq's short book on H.P. Lovecraft is the best criticism of that American author published so far anywhere.

The *Paix Liturgique* Report, in eight installments, is attributed to the late Daniel Hamiche and is largely structured as an interview between him and the publication. It deals primarily with the present and benefits from "field work": surveys on the current views of American Catholics. In certain areas the Report provides unique information— such as the installment on the sedevacantists and the independent priests. Given its French audience, the Report of necessity needs to set its discussion of traditionalism in the wider framework of American Catholicism, both past and present. The Report accordingly starts with a brief historical review of American Catholicism from the sixteenth century to Vatican II. Actually, I have more critical comments on certain factual statements and judgments in this installment as opposed to the content of later parts dealing with traditionalism itself.

For example, we read that "only two colonies, Maryland ... and Rhode Island (which practiced a 'blind welcome,' that is, without religious exclusion) had a Catholic population...." Rhode Island was actually militantly anti-Catholic. Perhaps the author really means Pennsylvania, the second British colony with a significant Catholic population, which just before the American Revolution was far more tolerant of Catholics than the original Catholic home of Maryland. Katherine Drexel was not a convert. Elizabeth Seton founded the Sisters of Charity in the United States, not just those of New York (that designation relates to a split later in the nineteenth century).

As one might expect, the Report describes with justifiable pride the major contribution of French Bishops in the early years of the US: some dioceses—New Orleans, Bardstown/Louisville, Vincennes/Indianapolis—were largely or totally in their hand, while Boston, New York, and Baltimore each had at least one French prelate. However, although I haven't attempted to make a complete tally, I am not totally sure that French bishops were a "majority" of the US episcopate in the first half of the nineteenth century.

Of more substance are some nuances that I don't think the author got exactly right. The domination of Irish Catholicism from 1830 onward is not attributable to the sudden appearance of the Irish: they always had been a strong component of American Catholicism from the founding of the United States. Rather, it was the radically increased number of the Irish (and also the German) immigrants in the decades preceding the Civil War that by 1860 transformed the Catholic Church in America from an exotic fringe to a significant presence at least in

most urban areas. The author also seems to think that
the status of Catholics as a "closed society" prior to the
Second Vatican Council is attributable to the multiplication
of ethnic parishes. That was hardly the case—the alleged
Catholic preconciliar "ghetto" was typified by the mainstream "American-Irish" parishes, not Italian or Polish
national churches.

Finally we note with some humor (and perplexity)
our author's assertion that: "One hears now and then
that American Catholics are more pious and practicing
(compared to those of Western Europe). . . . It's hardly
astonishing that 25% of baptized Catholics attend Mass
every Sunday and of the remaining 75% a good propor-
tion attends Protestant services, depending on the region."

Perhaps this level of religious practice is acceptable, even
admirable, compared to France or Germany—it is absolutely catastrophic, however, for the Catholic Church in
America and for its finances. And the author attributes even
these statistics primarily to the social pressure of an allegedly
Protestant society. Now, as indicated in the very quote above,
the Report is well aware of the "regional" differences in
the United States. I am not sure, though, that the author
fully appreciates how radical those differences can be. For
example, whatever the situation in "Trump country" may
be, no conformist pressure supporting religious practice
exists in any of the places that control the secular power in
the United States: New York City, Los Angeles, Washington
D. C., Chicago, Silicon Valley/San Francisco, the suburbs of
all these places, almost all of higher education—to name
only the most prominent examples. Indeed, in this stratum
of American society the public hostility to Christianity of
any kind is strong and growing ever stronger. Like many
European traditionalists, *Paix Liturgique* is perhaps a bit too
enthusiastic about the American scene.

The chapter of the Report on independent priests and sedevacantism is a unique contribution and fills a gap in my own essay. I would, however, wish to see the support for the author's estimate of the number of independent priests: it seems extraordinarily high to me. At least today in and around New York they are (perhaps with one exception) hardly found at all. The significant presence of various sedevacantist sects (as well as other FSSPX off-shoots) is duly noted, as is the fact that such movements seem more numerous in America than elsewhere. But, if we consider sedevacantism to be the flip side of extreme ultramontanism, does not the Irish, papalist heritage of the "American Catholic Church" explain this phenomenon?

I would also highlight the installments of the Report on traditionalism in the religious life, particularly that of the female religious. He also deals with the Society of St. John Cantius at some length. Yet in his enumeration of "traditional priests," he considers the FSSPX, the FSSP, and the ICRSS—who celebrate the traditional Mass exclusively—to be the sole "traditionalist" clergy of the United States. I have noticed this attitude in other European publications.

I have attended celebrations of the traditional Mass since 1988. Except in the very last year, almost all my experiences were with diocesan priests or members of mainstream religious orders who celebrated both the traditional Mass and the Novus Ordo. Thus this essay very much underestimates the actual scale of traditionalist activity. Of course the author is aware that there are a great many celebrations of the traditional Mass in addition to those of the above orders and dedicated traditionalist "chapels" (his term) and that many diocesan priests are involved. The author rightly points out the remarkable number of diocesan priests that have received training in the traditional rite. He seems to think, however, that the activities of the diocesan priests are a kind of underground. That has not been the case for many years—traditionalism in many places has become a normal aspect of American Catholic life.

Indeed, our author is heartened by his surveys that indicate that 72.7% of practicing Catholics find the simultaneous practice of both the Novus Ordo and the traditional Mass pursuant to *Summorum Pontificum* "normal" and that 41.5% of these Catholics could well see themselves attending the traditional Mass if it were offered at their parish. That's impressive testimony to how, in the United States at least, the traditional Mass has joined the mainstream of the Church as a significant and beneficial force. It is precisely for this reason, of course, that Pope Francis has now determined to destroy Catholic traditionalism. What will be the result of his campaign in the United States? The facts set forth in this essay, demonstrating the growing strength and acceptance of traditionalism among the laity, priests, and religious, give me some confidence that it will survive the trials that are to come.

Select Bibliography

THIS BIBLIOGRAPHY INCLUDES BOOKS THAT illustrate or fill in details about the American traditionalist movement as well as its enemies and affiliates. It also include a few more general titles written by influential members of this movement or parallel to it, but with a view to understanding the history. It does *not* include today's abundant new writing in explanation of or defense of Catholic tradition in general and the ancient Roman liturgy in particular. Extensive bibliographies of such works may be found, inter alia, in Peter Kwasniewski's *Resurgent in the Midst of Crisis*; *Noble Beauty, Transcendent Holiness*; and *Reclaiming Our Roman Catholic Birthright*.

Bethel, Fr. Francis, O.S.B. *John Senior and the Restoration of Realism*. Merrimack, NH: Thomas More College Press, 2016.

Bozell, L. Brent. *Mustard Seeds: A Conservative becomes a Catholic—Collected Essays*. Manassas, VA: Trinity Communications, 1986. [Includes many essays from *Triumph*.]

P.B.B. [Patricia Buckley Bozell], ed. *The Best of* Triumph. Front Royal, VA: Christendom Press, 2004. [Selected essays from the magazine.]

Buckley, Jr., William F. *Nearer, My God: An Autobiography of Faith*. Garden City, NY: Doubleday, 1997. [Good passages on the upheavals around Vatican II and on the phases of liturgical reform.]

Bullivant, Stephen. *Mass Exodus: Catholic Disaffiliation in Britain and America since Vatican II*. Oxford: Oxford University Press, 2019.

Carlin, David. *The Decline and Fall of the Catholic Church in America*. Manchester, NH: Sophia Institute Press, 2003.

Cowden-Guido, Richard. *John Paul II and the Battle for Vatican II*. Manassas, VA: Trinity Communications, 1986. [As perfect a statement of the "conservative" position as one could wish for; dedicated to then-auxiliary bishop Donald Wuerl.]

Day, Thomas. *Why Catholics Can't Sing: The Culture of Catholicism and the Triumph of Bad Taste*. New York, NY: Crossroad Publishing Company, 1990.

Darroch, Leo. *Una Voce: The History of the Foederatio Internationalis Una Voce 1964–2003*. Leominster, UK: Gracewing, 2017.

Dwyer, Archbishop Robert. *Ecclesiastes: The Book of Archbishop Robert Dwyer. A Selection of His Writings*. Edited by Albert J. Steiss. Second edition. Waterloo, ON: Arouca Press, 2021. [A participant in all the sessions of Vatican II, Dwyer wrote extensively about the issues the council raised, including in the area of liturgy, and what was going right—and wrong—in the US.]

Ferrara, Christopher, and Thomas E. Woods, Jr. *The Great Façade: The Regime of Novelty in the Catholic Church from Vatican II to the Francis Revolution*. Second edition. Kettering, OH: Angelico Press, 2015.

Golway, Terry, ed. *Catholics in New York: Society, Culture and Politics 1808–1946*. New York: Fordham University Press, 2008. [Actually discusses developments up to about 1970.]

Hamiche, Daniel. "Enquête sur la Tradition Catholique aux États-Unis" (2021). *Letters* 786, 787, 788, 790, 791, 792, 794, and 795 of *Paix Liturgique*. Accessed August 25, 2021.

Hartch, Todd. *A Time to Build Anew: How to Find the True, Good, and Beautiful in America*. Brooklyn, NY: Angelico Press, 2021. [Discusses a number of enterprises that originated in conservative and traditionalist Catholic circles in the US.]

Hildebrand, Dietrich von. *Trojan Horse in the City of God*. Chicago, IL: Franciscan Herald Press, 1967.

Hitchcock, James. *Catholicism and Modernity: Confrontation or Capitulation?* New York: The Seabury Press, 1979. [A conservative analysis of the state of ecclesial affairs ten years after the Novus Ordo was promulgated.]

Kelly, Daniel. *Living on Fire: The Life of L. Brent Bozell Jr.* Wilmington, Delaware: ISI Books, 2014.

Kelly, Msgr. George A. *The Battle for the American Church.* Garden
City, NY: Doubleday, 1979; reprinted by Image Books, 1981.
————. *Keeping the Church Catholic with John Paul II.* Garden
City, NY: Doubleday, 1990. [One of several less influential
follow-ups to *The Battle for the American Catholic Church* by
the same author.]

Larson, Anne M. *Love in the Ruins: Modern Catholics in Search
of the Ancient Faith.* Kansas City, MO: Angelus Press, 2009.
[The thirteen stories of pilgrimage to tradition are from
American writers.]

Martin, Malachi. *Windswept House. A Vatican Novel.* New York:
Doubleday, 1996. [This novel largely focuses on the American
Church. In many respects what we have learned about reality
since 1996 exceeds Martin's fiction!]

McCaffrey, Neil. *And Rightly So: Selected Letters and Articles of
Neil McCaffrey.* Edited by Peter A. Kwasniewski. Fort Col-
lins, CO: Roman Catholics Books, 2019. [Offers abundant
commentary on the conservative movement in America in the
50s, 60s, 70s, and 80s, with special attention to the enormous
wave of changes in the Catholic Church.]

McGinley, Brandon. *The Prodigal Church: Restoring Catholic
Tradition in an Age of Deception.* Manchester, NH: Sophia
Institute Press, 2020. [Part 1, "How We Got Here," probes
some of the strengths and weaknesses of the preconciliar
Church in America.]

McInerny, Ralph. *Connolly's Life.* New York: Atheneum, 1983. [A
novel that dramatizes the problems of post-Vatican II life in
the American Church.]
————. *What Went Wrong with Vatican II: The Catholic Crisis
Explained.* Manchester, NH: Sophia Institute Press, 1998.
[A well-intentioned but ultimately superficial account of the
Council and its aftermath, in this respect exemplifying the
conservative approach in general.]

Mitchell, Peter M. *The Coup at Catholic University: The 1968
Revolution in American Catholic Education.* San Francisco:
Ignatius Press, 2015.

Molnar, Thomas. *Ecumenism or New Reformation?* New York:
Funk & Wagnalls, 1968.

Pecklers, S.J., Keith F. *The Unread Vision: The Liturgical Movement in the United States of America: 1926–1955*. Collegeville, MN: The Liturgical Press, 1998.

Popowski, Mark D. *The Rise and Fall of* Triumph: *The History of a Radical Roman Catholic Magazine 1966–1976*. Lanham, MD: Lexington Books, 2012.

Priest, Where Is Thy Mass? Mass, Where Is Thy Priest? Seventeen Priests Tell Why They Celebrate the Latin Mass. Expanded edition. Kansas City, MO: Angelus Press, 2004.

Roche Muggeridge, Anne. *The Desolate City: Revolution in the Catholic Church*. Revised and expanded edition. New York: Harper & Row, 1990.

Senior, John. *The Remnants: The Final Essays of John Senior*. Edited by Andrew Senior. Forest Lake, MN: The Remnant Press, 2013.

Sheehan, Edward R.F. *Cardinal Galsworthy. A Novel*. New York: Viking, 1997.

Steichen, Donna. *Ungodly Rage: The Hidden Face of Catholic Feminism*. San Francisco: Ignatius Press, 1991. [Much of the content concerns events and trends in the Church in the United States.]

Storck, Thomas. *From Christendom to Americanism and Beyond: The Long, Jagged Trail to a Postmodern Void*. Kettering, OH: Angelico Press, 2015.

Tracy, Bishop Robert E. *American Bishop at the Vatican Council*. New York: McGraw-Hill, 1966. [The chapter on the liturgy makes for eye-opening reading.]

Vatican Secretariat of State, *Report on the Holy See's Institutional Knowledge and Decision-Making Related to Former Cardinal Theodore Edgar McCarrick (1930 to 2017)*. Vatican City State, November 10, 2020. [While this report has been roundly criticized for its self-serving aspects, it has valuable documentation on the state of the Roman Catholic Church in the United States in the period it covers.]

Wills, Garry. *Bare Ruined Choirs: Doubt, Prophecy, and Radical Religion*. Garden City, NY: Doubleday, 1972. [The titles of the book's parts describe the author's view of the Church: Changeless; Changing; Doubting; Dying; Hoping. His treatment of "Fifties Catholicism" is worthy of study.]

STUART CHESSMAN has been a financial executive with several large multinational corporations. Since 2007 he has been a leader of the Society of St. Hugh of Cluny, which is dedicated to the preservation and spread of the Traditional Latin Mass. Mr. Chessman is married and has five children. He resides in Connecticut.

CPSIA information can be obtained
at www.ICGtesting.com
Printed in the USA
LVHW031915030322
712535LV00005B/102/J